Hand Me Another Brick
Bible Companion

Timeless Lessons on Leadership

Hand Me Another Brick
Bible Companion

Timeless Lessons on Leadership

BASED ON THE BOOK BY

CHARLES R. SWINDOLL

Produced in association with CREATIVE MINISTRIES
Insight for Living

THOMAS NELSON
Since 1798

NASHVILLE   DALLAS   MEXICO CITY   RIO DE JANEIRO   BEIJING

HAND ME ANOTHER BRICK
Timeless Lessons on Leadership

Bible Companion

Published by W Publishing Group, a division of Thomas Nelson, Inc., Post Office Box 141000, Nashville, Tennessee, 37214.

Published in association with Yates & Yates, LLP, Attorneys and Counselors, Orange, California.

Editorial Staff: Nelson Impact, a Division of Thomas Nelson, Inc.
Cover Design: Tobias' Outerwear for Books

W Publishing Group books may be purchased in bulk for educational, business, fund-raising, or sales promotional use. For information, please email: SpecialMarkets@ThomasNelson.com.

ISBN-13: 978-1-4185-2751-8
Printed in the United States of America

09 10 11 12 -- 9 8 7 6 5 4 3 2

DISCOVERING THE WAY explores the principles of Scripture through observation and interpretation of the Bible passages and drawing out practical principles for life. Parallel passages and additional questions supplement the main Scriptures for a more in-depth study.

 STARTING YOUR JOURNEY focuses on application to help you put into practice the principles of the lesson in ways that fit your personality, gifts, and level of spiritual maturity.

USING THE BIBLE COMPANION

Hand Me Another Brick Bible Companion is designed with both individual study and small-group use in mind. Here's the method we recommend:

Prayer—Begin each lesson with prayer, asking God to teach you through His Word and to open your heart to the self-discovery afforded by the questions and text of the lesson.

Scripture—Have your Bible handy. We recommend the New American Standard Bible or another literal translation, rather than a paraphrase. As you progress through each lesson, the reading icon will prompt you to read relevant sections of Scripture. You will also want to look up Scripture passages noted in parentheses.

Questions—As you encounter the questions, approach them wisely and creatively. Not every question will be applicable to every person all the time. Use the questions as general guides in your thinking rather than rigid forms

How to Use This
Bible Companion

L*eadership.* The word stirs excitement in some and abhorrence in others. Some regard it with eagerness and ambition, others with fear and trepidation. But whether we like to admit it or not, we're all in leadership of some form. Whether we run a major corporation, issue orders in an army unit, or shepherd a child in Sunday school, we're responsible for guiding and leading others in some realm of our lives. That's why we can all benefit from a study of Nehemiah's legendary leadership.

Whether you choose to complete this study individually or as part of a group, a brief introduction to the overall structure of each lesson will help you get the most out of these lessons.

LESSON ORGANIZATION

THE HEART OF THE MATTER highlights the main idea of each lesson for rapid orientation. The lesson itself is then composed of two main teaching sections for insight and application:

A Letter from Chuck

In the fast-paced, highly competitive world of twenty-first century leadership, many of us are overdue for a fresh word from God on the matter. How much we need His steady, unchanging wisdom in our world of Web meetings, sixty-hour workweeks, and corporate scandal!

Though projects and people change with every generation, the principles of godly leadership remain the same. That's why we need the ancient book of Nehemiah. It may be ancient, but it is not out of date! It continues to speak to those of us in leadership today. Whether you run a business or a home, serve in ministry, government, education, or the military . . . the book of Nehemiah provides timely and timeless tools for leadership.

Unlike the dog-eat-dog mentality of our day, Nehemiah models a rare blend of godliness, tact, discipline, determination, grace, and objectivity. You'll admire his remarkable management skills, and at the same time, you'll smile at the way he handles criticism. His project? The building of a wall around Jerusalem. His work force? An unlikely conglomeration of people—some skilled, most not at all—who needed motivation, direction, and encouragement. In one word, they needed *leadership*. And that's exactly what he provided . . . in abundance.

My hope is that each lesson in this Bible Companion will minister to you in your realm of leadership as you apply the wisdom of the Word and then watch God work!

CHUCK SWINDOLL

CONTENTS

CONTENTS

BOOKS FOR ADULTS, CONT'D

Suddenly One Morning
Swindoll's Ultimate Book of Illustrations
   and Quotes
The Tale of the Tardy Oxcart
Three Steps Forward, Two Steps Back

Victory: A Winning Game Plan for Life
Why, God?
Wisdom for the Way
You and Your Child

MINIBOOKS

Abraham: A Model of Pioneer Faith
David: A Model of Pioneer Courage
Esther: A Model of Pioneer Independence

Moses: A Model of Pioneer Vision
Nehemiah: A Model of Pioneer
   Determination

BOOKLETS

Anger
Attitudes
Commitment
Dealing with Defiance
Demonism
Destiny
Divorce
Eternal Security
Forgiving and Forgetting
Fun Is Contagious!
God's Will
Hope
Impossibilities
Integrity
Intimacy with the Almighty
Leisure
The Lonely Whine of the Top Dog
Make Your Dream Come True

Making the Weak Family Strong
Moral Purity
Peace . . . in Spite of Panic
Portrait of a Faithful Father
The Power of a Promise
Prayer
Reflections from the Heart—
   A Prayer Journal
Seeking the Shepherd's Heart—
   A Prayer Journal
Sensuality
Stress
This Is No Time for Wimps
Tongues
When Your Comfort Zone Gets the Squeeze
Woman

BOOKS FOR CHILDREN

Paw Paw Chuck's Big Ideas in the Bible

HAND ME ANOTHER BRICK
Timeless Lessons on Leadership

Bible Companion

From the Bible-Teaching Ministry of Charles R. Swindoll

Charles R. Swindoll has devoted his life to the clear, practical teaching and application of God's Word and His grace. A pastor at heart, Chuck has served as senior pastor to congregations in Texas, Massachusetts, and California. He currently pastors Stonebriar Community Church in Frisco, Texas, but Chuck's listening audience extends far beyond a local church body. As a leading program in Christian broadcasting, *Insight for Living* airs in major Christian radio markets around the world, reaching people groups in languages they can understand. Chuck's extensive writing ministry has also served the body of Christ worldwide and his leadership as president and now chancellor of Dallas Theological Seminary has helped prepare and equip a new generation for ministry. Chuck and Cynthia, his partner in life and ministry, have four grown children and ten grandchildren.

Based upon the original outlines, charts, and transcripts of Charles R. Swindoll's sermons, the study guide text originally co-authored by Lee Hough titled *Hand Me Another Brick: A Study of Nehemiah* was re-titled *Hand Me Another Brick: Timeless Lessons on Leadership* and was revised and expanded as a Bible Companion by Michael J. Svigel, Th.M., Ph.D. candidate, Dallas Theological Seminary.

Editor in Chief: Cynthia Swindoll, President, Insight for Living
Executive Vice President: Wayne Stiles, Th.M., D. Min., Dallas Theological Seminary
Director of Creative Ministries: Michael J. Svigel, Th.M., Ph.D. candidate, Dallas Theological Seminary
Content Editors: Brie Engeler, B.A., University Scholars, Baylor University; Amy L. Snedaker, B.A., English, Rhodes College
Copy Editor: Jim Craft, M.A., English, Mississippi College
Project Coordinator, Creative Ministries: Cari Harris, B.A., Journalism, Grand Canyon University
Collaborative material was provided by the Creative Ministries Department.

An effort has been made to locate sources and obtain permission where necessary for the quotations used in this book. In the event of any unintentional omission, a modification will gladly be incorporated in future printings.

to complete. If there are things you just don't understand or that you want to explore further, be sure to jot down your thoughts or questions.

A SPECIAL NOTE FOR SMALL GROUPS

If you have chosen to complete this study in a small-group setting, carefully consider the following suggestions.

Preparation—All group members should try to prepare in advance by working through the lessons as described in the previous section. If you serve as the leader, you should take additional steps to supplement your preparation either by listening to the corresponding sermons (available for purchase at www.insight.org), reading the book, *Hand Me Another Brick*, by Charles R. Swindoll, or by reading any of the recommended resources listed at the back of this book. Mastery of the material will build your confidence and competence, and approaching the topic from various perspectives will equip you to freely guide discussion.

Discussion Questions—You should feel free to mold the lesson according to the needs of your unique group. While planning the lesson, you will want to mark questions you feel fit the time allotment, needs, and interests of your group. Not all questions will work for all groups, so be creative.

Flexibility—During group time, open in prayer, then lead the group through the lesson you planned in advance. Members may want to share their own answers to the questions, contribute their insights, or steer the discussion in a particular direction that fits the needs of the group. Sometimes group members will want to discuss questions you may have left out of the planned lesson. *Be flexible*, but try to stay on schedule so the group has sufficient time for the final section, "Starting Your Journey," where the application of the lesson begins.

Goal—If it's unrealistic for your group to complete an entire lesson during a session, consider continuing where you left off in the next session. The goal is not merely to cover material, but to promote in-depth, personal discussion of the topic with a view toward personal response and application. To do this, the group will need both to understand the biblical principles and to apply them to their lives.

Our prayer is that this Insight for Living Bible Companion will not only help you to dig deeper into what God's Word says about biblical leadership, but that you will also glean insights and application for real life.

SPECIAL BIBLE COMPANION FEATURES

Throughout the chapters, you'll find several special features designed to add insight or depth to your study. Use these features to enhance your study and deepen your knowledge of Scripture, history, and theology.

GETTING TO THE ROOT

While our English versions of the Scriptures are reliable, studying the original languages can often bring to light nuances of the text that are sometimes missed in translation. This feature explores the meaning of the underlying Hebrew or Greek words or phrases in a particular passage, sometimes providing parallel examples to illuminate the meaning of the inspired text.

DIGGING DEEPER

Various passages in Scripture touch on deeper theological questions or confront modern worldviews and philosophies that conflict with a biblical worldview. This feature will help you gain deeper insight into specific theological issues related to the biblical text.

DOORWAY TO HISTORY

Sometimes the chronological gap that separates us from the original author and readers clouds our understanding of a passage of Scripture. This feature takes you back in time to explore the surrounding history, culture, and customs of the world in which Nehemiah was written.

LESSON ONE

The Matter at Hand

Survey of Nehemiah

THE HEART OF THE MATTER

In his roles as cupbearer, builder, and governor, Nehemiah exemplified the qualities of a wise, godly leader. Regardless of the extent of our own realm of leadership or the skills and experiences we bring to the table, we can learn from Nehemiah's example as we examine our own character and God-given place in life. Like the bricks and mortar of a solid, ancient city wall, the bricks of excellent leadership must be placed on a foundation of the Bible and godly character with the mortar of faith and fortitude.

DISCOVERING THE WAY

Remember this line? "Little pig, little pig, let me come in, or I'll huff and I'll puff and I'll blow your house in!" Who can forget that blustery threat from the fang-toothed villain of bedtime stories, the big, bad wolf? You know the story. The wolf *did* blow down the homes of the first two little pigs, but the third little pig had prepared well. His patient planning and perseverance paid off. Not only did he save himself, but he also provided protection for his foolish brothers. They had taken the quick and easy route, building their homes from weak materials.

When it comes to leadership qualities, do you build with the hay and twigs of worldly strategies or with the solid and enduring Word of God? If you find that your leadership principles keep collapsing with the slightest wind of change, you need to take a long, hard look at Nehemiah's example. The wall he built around Jerusalem represented more than stones and mortar. It rose from rock-solid leadership traits that developed in the midst of struggle and opposition.

As we study Nehemiah's life, we'll see that many difficulties and trials came knocking on his door, threatening to blow his house down, as they do ours. Criticism . . . discouragement . . . financial problems . . . lack of motivation. He saw it all. But those gusts of resistance couldn't blow him down. Nor could they stop him from leading his people to rebuild Jerusalem's walls—walls that would provide protection against the wolves that threatened God's returning remnant in the land of Israel.

What would you say are your major realms of leadership today? Remember, leadership can take place in the home, in a business, in a ministry, or in another organization—any situation in which a group of people looks to you for guidance.

Who are the specific people under your leadership? Identify them by name.

_____

_____

_____

_____

_____

In twenty-five words or less, how would you summarize your primary mission, the most important task you're trying to accomplish in your realms of leadership?

_____

_____

_____

As you work through the lessons in this Bible Companion, keep these people and this task in mind. The Holy Spirit inspired Nehemiah to record his experiences for a purpose. Though Nehemiah's people and project were unique, the problems he faced are universal. And the same strategies that strengthened Nehemiah's leadership will help fortify yours.

HISTORICAL EVENTS RELATED TO NEHEMIAH'S DAY

In order to fully appreciate Nehemiah's leadership, we need to understand the existing historical situation during which God called him to his task.

All Jewish history flows down from one individual, Abraham, whom God promised to make into a great nation that would bless the world from their own land (Genesis 12:1–3). Centuries later, under the reigns of Saul, David, and Solomon, the dawn of God's glorious promises to Abraham began to peek over the horizon. But, like a lingering, arctic dawn that never turns to day, poor leadership—resulting from poor character—delayed their fulfillment.

During Solomon's reign, his moral compromises became so great that God finally judged him (1 Kings 11:11–12). In 931 BC, the ten northern tribes revolted and formed their own nation, Israel. The two remaining tribes in the south bore the name of Judah. The corrupt leadership of the northern kingdom embraced pagan idolatry for the next two centuries, and in 722 BC God removed this corrupted branch of Abraham's offspring, using the Assyrians as His tool of judgment.

In the south, Judah was blessed with a number of wise, godly leaders who launched several revivals among the people, rebuilding the crumbling leadership of predecessors and returning the people to the Lord and His Law. However, the kings of Judah eventually turned away from the Lord, and from 606 to 586 BC, the Babylonians first tormented, then destroyed Jerusalem—including the temple and the city walls (2 Chronicles 36:17–20). While the city itself had been wisely built with stones, those in leadership had inner foundations of sticks and straw. The people of Judah were taken as captives to Babylon, where God continued to preserve a faithful remnant among His people.

After an appointed time of seventy years, God shifted the balance of world power from the Babylonians to the Persians and Medes. He then prompted the new captors to allow the Jews to return to their homeland. First King Cyrus, and later Artaxerxes, allowed the Jews to return home and to pick up the pieces of their ravaged lives and land (2 Chronicles 36:22–23; Ezra 7:11–13). The first band of returnees, led by Zerubbabel in 536 BC, focused on rebuilding the temple. The second band, led by Ezra in 457 BC, focused on rebuilding the spiritual lives of the people. Finally, in 444 BC, Nehemiah returned to rebuild the walls needed to protect the remnant of Israel from the outside forces bent on destroying them.

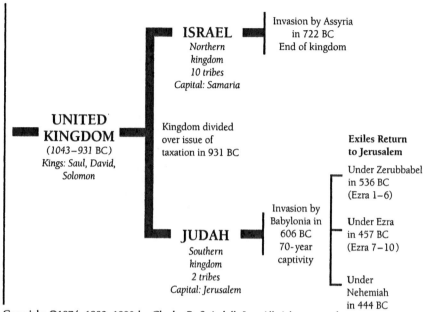

NEHEMIAH: THE MAN OF THE HOUR

Nehemiah's leadership revealed itself in three successive roles he played: cupbearer, builder, and governor. Each position adds an important element of perspective on his leadership qualities and reveals that solid, godly principles of leadership are applicable regardless of one's position.

First, Nehemiah served in the role of cupbearer to King Artaxerxes of Persia (Nehemiah 1:11). This high office placed Nehemiah in an unparalleled position of continual and personal access to the king. During this time of service, Nehemiah received devastating news concerning Jerusalem's broken walls (1:1–3). Instead of taking advantage of his place in the presence of the king, however, Nehemiah took his heartfelt petition for the rebuilding of Jerusalem to the King of kings in prayer (1:4–11).

DOORWAY TO HISTORY

The Cupbearer

In ancient royal palaces, the cupbearer was far more than just a robed servant, butler, or slave. He was entrusted with the responsibility of tasting the king's food and drink to make sure it was not poisoned. In such an important, self-sacrificing role, the cupbearer often enjoyed great trust and confidence in the Near Eastern royal courts.[1] One writer notes that the cupbearer "in ancient oriental courts was always a person of rank and importance. From the confidential nature of his duties and his frequent access to the royal presence, he possessed great influence."[2]

Eventually, Nehemiah's countenance began to reflect the strain of carrying his burden for Jerusalem in his heart, and the king noticed (Nehemiah 2:1–4). God provided an answer to Nehemiah's prayers. With the king's permission, Nehemiah laid aside his prestigious cupbearer's robes and put on a hard hat to assume his new role as Nehemiah the builder (2:5–10).

What unique advantages can you imagine Nehemiah enjoyed in his role as cupbearer?

_____

_____

_____

_____

As you consider your own realms of leadership, what unique advantages and privileged relationships do you enjoy?

_____

_____

_____

How can these privileges be both a blessing and a burden? Spend some time considering the positives and negatives of your position.

_____

_____

_____

The second role Nehemiah played in this chronicle was that of a builder. Upon his arrival in Jerusalem, his first task was to inspect the ruins of the wall and form a strategy for reconstruction (Nehemiah 2:11–15). (See the map on page 39.) After his moonlit survey to size up the task before him, Nehemiah readied himself to bring his plans to the people (2:17–18). Chapters 3 through 5 describe the work they carried out in spite of great odds, obstacles, and enemies. But eventually the people's prayers, planning, and perseverance resulted in a strong defensive wall.

What character qualities are illustrated by Nehemiah's attitudes, words, and actions in the following passages? Give one or two descriptive words for each passage.

Nehemiah 2:1–2

_____

Nehemiah 2:4; 4:4–5

_____

Nehemiah 2:5

_____

Nehemiah 2:12, 16

_____

Nehemiah 2:18

_____

Nehemiah 2:20

_____

Nehemiah 4:14

_____

Nehemiah 5:6–7, 13

_____

Based on this overview, if somebody were to ask you what Nehemiah was like as a person, how would you describe him?

_____

_____

_____

As both cupbearer and builder, Nehemiah drew from his godly character and faith in God's promises. Next, Nehemiah laid his hard hat aside to take up the keys to the city and begin functioning in his new role as governor (Nehemiah 5:14). As his first official task in this appointed position, Nehemiah commissioned spiritual men to occupy places of authority in the city (7:1–2). He also reestablished the practicing of God's laws and purified the people from harmful foreign influences (13:30). Nehemiah would long be remembered "for good, according to all that [he had] done for this people" (5:19).

STARTING YOUR JOURNEY

Ancient walls served many functions. They offered protection and security, and they reflected the strength of the people. They also made it possible for the people to cultivate their spiritual lives nationally as well as individually without outside interference.

The kind of godly, wise leadership that shone forth from Nehemiah's life does not come from suddenly plugging into an instant power source. It is built with deliberate strength and intensity through years of putting faith to work. Before we look at Nehemiah's struggle to rebuild Jerusalem's walls, maybe we need to examine the condition of our own spiritual walls. Have some gates been left open for the enemy to slip through? Have the weeds of compromise overrun certain sections until toppled stones have become main thoroughfares for rebellion?

If your personal walls of spiritual discipline are in need of repair—whether merely a brick or two or even an entire section—take a moment now to apply some of the principles Nehemiah's life offers.

First, Concern for Character. *Develop a genuine concern for the condition of the walls.* The work to restore the walls of Jerusalem didn't start when the people began laying bricks. It began as a burden in one man's heart. Like Nehemiah, we must have a genuine concern for the condition of the walls in our own lives.

Second, Foundation of Prayer. *Express direct prayer for guidance and protection.* Before he ever began to rebuild the wall, Nehemiah started working on it from eight hundred miles away—in prayer before the Lord. For many of us, prayer is too often an afterthought, something rattled off at ribbon cuttings when the work has already been done. Get in the habit of acting on your burdens only *after* you have given them a firm foundation of prayer.

Third, Spirit of Determination. *Face the situation honestly and with determination until the task is finished.* When Nehemiah met with the people of Jerusalem, he didn't attempt to gloss over the true condition of the walls (Nehemiah 2:17). Only through an honest appraisal could he secure the kind of steadfast commitment it would take to see the job finished. Likewise, without an honest appraisal of our own spiritual condition, we will always run out of determination and motivation before the gaps are filled.

Fourth, Attitude of Humility. *Recognize that we cannot correct the condition by ourselves.* Our natural tendency is to retreat alone into a spiritual wilderness. But only when we are willing to live in dependence upon God and in humility toward others will we have the power to erect the spiritual fortification we need for protection and for fulfilling the roles of leadership God has given to us.

Recalling the people and projects you identified as your primary realms of leadership, answer the following questions prayerfully.

Review the four principles described above, and choose one from the diagram that you feel most impacts the people and projects in your current realms of leadership. Within the diagram, describe how and why this principle is the most important to your specific leadership role.

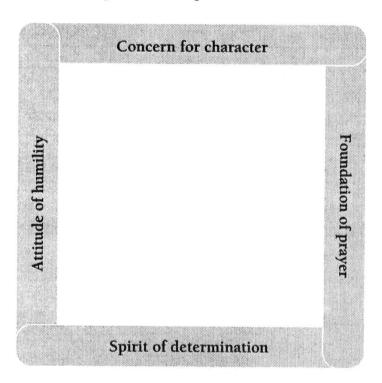

If an enemy were to attack your spiritual walls, which of these four principles would show the most weakness and neglect? Why?

_____

_____

Write a simple prayer, asking God to begin repairing and strengthening your spiritual walls, focusing on both the most important and the weakest areas. Spend a few moments bringing your concerns directly to Him.

_____

_____

_____

_____

_____

_____

_____

_____

_____

The walls of spiritual strength we build around our lives protect us and help us to cultivate a strong relationship with the Lord. Throughout this Bible Companion, when we examine the various leadership roles that Nehemiah filled, we will reflect on our own leadership styles with the objectivity that comes as we align ourselves with the standard of God's Word. Are you ready to step up to the challenge?

NEHEMIAH

	Cupbearer to the King	Builder of the Wall	Governor of the People	
	Prayer May I? You may!	"So the wall was completed . . . in 52 days." (6:15)	Scripture found (7:5) read (8:3–7) explained (8:8) — Lives changed (8:1–3, 9; 10:28–31) — Nation confronted and cleansed (13:10–30) Prayer	
	CHAPTERS 1:1–2:10	CHAPTERS 2:11–6:19	CHAPTERS 7–13	
Location	Susa, Persia	Jerusalem in Palestine		
Focus	Leadership of a man	Revival of a nation		
Subject	Burden	Project	Scriptures	Reforms
Difficulties	The King	Enemies	Tradition	Compromises
Victories	Release	Accomplishment	Obedience	Changes
Theme	Nehemiah's trust in the covenant-keeping God			
Key Verse	6:15–16; 8:8–10; 9			
Christ in Nehemiah	Suggested in Nehemiah, who leaves an exalted position to identify with the plight of his people and lead them into restoration. Pictured in Nehemiah's prayerful dependence on God.			

LESSON TWO

A Leader—From the Knees Up!

Nehemiah 1:1–11

THE HEART OF THE MATTER

Few Old Testament characters surpass Nehemiah in the potency of their *leadership*. God used him to motivate and direct a relatively small group of people in building a wall around the city of Jerusalem and then to establish a godly government. In this lesson we focus our attention on the first chapter of the book in which Nehemiah discovers Jerusalem's desperate need and then brings it before God in prayer. It is highly significant that the *first* place we find this great leader is *on his knees.*

DISCOVERING THE WAY

Sometimes in the unsophisticated but painfully honest world of children, we find the best answers to weighty questions such as, "What is leadership?" For example, remember how you resolved leadership struggles when you were a kid? You tried to entice other kids by saying, "Come play at my house. We have cake and ice cream!" Then the wide-eyed bunch spun around to hear a competing offer from another kid: "Oh yeah? Well, my mom just finished makin' some *biiiig* chocolate chip cookies—*and*—you can all ride my horse." End of leadership crisis. His horse trumped your cake. The barefoot electorate voted with a unanimous whoop and stampeded for their new leader's hacienda. You started to say something about your dad's jet, but it was too late.

When you apply the question, "What is leadership?" to that scene, one word comes to mind—*influence*. We lead people according to the degree that we influence them. From neighborhood politics to world politics, this one-word definition of leadership holds true. Leaders from different realms, nations, and neighborhoods agree: the stronger the influence, the stronger the leadership.

But how do we gain that influence? By offering the most cake and ice cream? By relying on manipulation techniques? Carrying the biggest club? Screaming the loudest? Throughout history, people have tried them all. And they all fall short of God's design for leadership. Only His method moves and influences people the way a true leader should.

What makes a great leader? List two or three characteristics or practices that identify great leaders.

Have you ever worked or served with a great leader? Describe your experience.

_____

_____

Why do you classify this person as a great leader? What did you learn from him or her?

_____

_____

_____

_____

Based on your answers, do you think that those who serve under your leadership would regard you as a great leader? Why, or why not?

_____

_____

_____

_____

A PRELUDE OF PRAYER

The book of Nehemiah contains a stockpile of leadership strategies and tactics that can and should be carefully incorporated into our lives. In the first chapter of his chronicle, Nehemiah offers the cornerstone on which the effective leader's influence truly rests—*prayer*.

 Read Nehemiah 1:1–3.

Without fanfare, Nehemiah identified himself as the book's author and later as King Artaxerxes's cupbearer (Nehemiah 1:1, 11). In this trusted position, Nehemiah acted as a protective screen between the public and the king. In addition, we are told that the action starts in the month of *Chislev*, or December, in the "twentieth year" of the king's reign, about 444 BC. We're also told that Nehemiah lived in Susa, the capital of Persia and much of the civilized world at that time. In this setting, Nehemiah lived out his normal, day-to-day routine. But it was all about to change.

Nehemiah may have lived in the Persian capital, but the capital of his heart was Jerusalem. One day, witnesses from Jerusalem relayed that the people in Nehemiah's homeland were in a calamitous, miserable, and depressing situation (Nehemiah 1:2–3). They suffered criticism and harassment from their enemies, lived in constant fear of attack, and—like the crumbled wall that surrounded them—their spiritual lives were in ruins.

How do you tend to respond to unexpected news? With panic or peace? Or perhaps anger or agitation? Why do you think you react this way?

_____

_____

_____

How do your responses to unpleasant reports affect those who work or serve under your leadership? Be specific.

_____

_____

_____

_____

Read Nehemiah 1:4–11.

Nehemiah played the first three verses of this concerto on leadership in a minor key. The introductory notes of verse 1 quickly segued into the dissonant tones of verses 2 and 3. Together, this overture of sorrowful strains struck a deep, resonant chord in Nehemiah's heart that flowed out in an arpeggio of verbs: "Nehemiah heard . . . sat . . . wept . . . mourned . . . fast[ed] . . . pray[ed]" (Nehemiah 1:4). And the main melody of verses 4–11 highlights four vital themes from Nehemiah's life, each a quality that should be found in the lives of true spiritual leaders.

First, *Nehemiah clearly recognized the need.* The beginnings of this theme are barely audible in the simple opening line: "When I heard these words" (Nehemiah 1:4). Although he worked in a palace, Nehemiah did not allow his heart or mind the luxury of ivory-tower preoccupations. He was not afraid to see the *real* problems, especially when it came to hearing about the needs of those closest to his heart.

Contrast Nehemiah's ability to identify real needs with the inability of Eli to do the same in 1 Samuel 2:12–16 and 3:11–13.

_____

_____

_____

_____

Examine your own realms of leadership. Are you deliberately choosing to ignore an issue or need? What is it? Why do you ignore it?

_____

_____

_____

_____

Second, *Nehemiah was personally concerned with the need.* The low, melodious tones of recognition suddenly gave way to the thunderous volume of remorse: "I sat down and wept, and mourned for many days" (Nehemiah 1:4). The rhythm of intense sorrow boomed and a steady shower of intense feelings ensued: "I was fasting and praying before the God of heaven" (1:4).

Nehemiah allowed the anguish and misery of his people to pierce his heart. And from that wound, Nehemiah's mourning for his people, along with his passion, were poured out in sonorous refrain before the Lord. Alan Redpath, in his book on Nehemiah, writes:

> Let us learn this lesson from Nehemiah: you never lighten the load unless you first have felt the pressure in your own soul. You are never used of God to bring blessing until God has opened your eyes and made you see things as they are. There is no other preparation for Christian work than that. Nehemiah was called to build the wall, but first he had to weep over the ruins.[1]

The typical leader's response would have been to blame the people: "They've been back for how long and still haven't built that wall? Who's in charge there? I want *names*!" But in Nehemiah's response we hear no discordant notes of blame—only the resonant notes of compassion and a willingness to get involved.

Do you know of someone within your realms of influence who has a need? How willing are you to get involved? Do you tend to react to such situations with apathy, irritability, blame, or compassion? Do others have needs that you may be overlooking or ignoring?

_____

_____

_____

_____

What does Philippians 2:3–4 say to you regarding these needs? How should you be responding to them?

_____

_____

_____

_____

Third, *Nehemiah brought the need to God first.* The third theme picks up on the final sweeping crescendo of verse 4: "I was . . . praying before the God of heaven." His heartfelt petition is recorded in verses 5–11, and here Nehemiah displayed the essence of his leadership. He resisted the normal temptation to pick up the conductor's baton and orchestrate the reparation of the wall himself. Instead, he fell on his knees, beseeching the One whose place it is to conduct all the affairs of men and to meld their efforts into one harmonious plan.

Take several minutes to study Nehemiah 1:5–11. Use the following questions to examine the praise, confession, promises, and petition in Nehemiah's powerful prayer.

According to verse 5, why did Nehemiah praise God?

_____

_____

In verses 6–7, why did Nehemiah make a confession? Be specific.

_____

_____

_____

Nehemiah trusted God for several promises in verses 8–10. List them here, and then compare them with those given in Leviticus 26:33 and Deuteronomy 30:1–5.

_____

_____

_____

According to verse 11, what did Nehemiah ask God to do?

_____

_____

Fourth, *Nehemiah was available to meet the need.* With this final theme, the overture of leadership reaches its finale. Amid the climactic strains of Nehemiah's petition (Nehemiah 1:11), an essential leadership quality emerges: *availability.* But in order to be available to meet the need of rebuilding the wall, Nehemiah had to overcome a hurdle: King Artaxerxes. This brings us back to the opening premise of our study: the primary importance of prayer in leadership. As we will see in the next lesson, only God has the power to mold and move the heart of a king.

STARTING YOUR JOURNEY

Our study of Nehemiah 1 leaves us with at least four reasons why prayer is not only important but vital in leadership. First, *prayer makes us wait.* We can't earnestly pray and at the same time rush ahead of God with rash actions. Prayer forces us to take a breath, adjust our attitudes before the Lord, and then act. Second, *prayer clears our vision.* It enables us to see the situation through God's eyes and not our own. Third, *prayer quiets our hearts.* We cannot continue to worry and pray at the same time. One will snuff out the other, depending on which one we choose. Fourth, *prayer activates our faith.* And with that faith comes an attitude of hope and peace that replaces the petty and critical attitude that is evident when we haven't spent time in prayer.

Great leadership begins with heartfelt, genuine submission to the headship of the Divine Leader. We express this submission by offering all our worries, concerns, challenges, hopes, and disappointments to God through prayer.

Consider the leadership struggles, challenges, and concerns you identified throughout this lesson. What is the single most pressing concern you are facing today in relation to your realms of leadership and those who follow you?

_____

_____

Are you struggling with the temptation to worry about this issue? Why, or why not?

_____

_____

According to Philippians 4:6, what is your alternative to anxiety?

_____

What does Philippians 4:7 promise to those who choose prayer instead of worry?

_____

Write a prayer bringing your concern before the Lord, incorporating all four parts of Nehemiah's prayer: praise, confession, promise, and petition.

_____

_____

_____

_____

_____

_____

_____

In this lesson we witnessed how Nehemiah wisely discerned the real needs of his people and brought them boldly before God's throne. Great leadership begins by submitting to the leadership of our great God. We express our submission by offering all of our concerns to Him through prayer and then trusting Him to care for them according to His perfect will. Do you want to be a great leader? Become a person of prayer.

LESSON THREE

Preparation for a Tough Job

Nehemiah 2:1–11

THE HEART OF THE MATTER

While carrying his great burden for the people and conditions in Jerusalem, Nehemiah began the mighty task of rebuilding the walls of Jerusalem by getting on his knees, asking God for compassion and understanding in the heart of King Artaxerxes (Nehemiah 1:11). In the second chapter of Nehemiah, we see God's gracious answer to Nehemiah's prayer, an illustration of Proverbs 21:1, and the launch of an incredible reconstruction project.

DISCOVERING THE WAY

An appropriate subtitle for this lesson could be, "How to Handle a Difficult Boss." Almost every person *in* leadership today is also *under* leadership—or at least accountable to a board of directors. One of the best ways to be a great leader is to learn how to be a great follower. And for those of us who strive to be good, faithful followers, we know it isn't always easy.

Describe a situation in your past employment or project in which you had to handle a difficult or mercurial boss. Recall the emotions, attitudes, words, and even actions that this experience produced in you. How did you respond? What was the ultimate result of this experience?

_____

_____

_____

_____

What words might those under your leadership use to describe your demeanor? Is it possible that anyone has perceived you as a tyrant?

_____

_____

A PRINCIPLE FROM PROVERBS

In our last lesson, one banner of truth waved high above all others. As Hudson Taylor, the great pioneer missionary to China, discovered, it is possible "to move man, through God, by prayer alone!"[1] Another pioneer, Nehemiah, also learned of the power of prayer to persuade others. When he faced a boss who seemed impossibly immobile, he applied this timeless principle from Scripture.

The first half of Proverbs 21:1 says, "The king's heart is like channels of water in the hand of the LORD." The word *channels* refers to canals or irrigation ditches that run in various directions from a main source of water. The writer says that the king's heart—the center of his will, intellect, and emotions, the place where all decisions are made—is under God's sovereign control. The second half of this proverb comes in the form of a declaration: "He turns it wherever He wishes." Whether the person in charge is a believer or not, whether he or she consciously submits to the commands of God or shakes a fist in rebellion against Him, the sovereign God ultimately deter-mines the direction in which the decisions of his or her heart will flow.

This verse from Proverbs 21 forms a perfect prologue to the drama in Nehemiah 2. Nehemiah served as the cupbearer to a dictator infamous for his rigid and stubborn will—a tough boss! The distressing news of Jerusalem's defenseless position raised in Nehemiah an urgent desire to rebuild his city's walls. He knew Artaxerxes was unlikely to give him leave. So he did the only thing he could do: He started praying.

Read the account of earlier letters sent to and from King Artaxerxes in Ezra 4:11–22. Assuming Nehemiah was aware of this correspondence, how do you think he viewed the king's attitude toward Jerusalem?

_____

_____

NEHEMIAH IN PERSIA

Through Nehemiah's personal account, we're given front-row seats in a dramatization of Proverbs 21:1, "The king's heart is like channels of water in the hand of the LORD; He turns it wherever He wishes." The events of Nehemiah 1 occurred in December, while the action in Nehemiah 2 took place in the month of *Nisan,* or April. In between were four anguishing months of praying and waiting.

The first verses of Nehemiah 2 record what is known in narratives as an *interchange*—the back-and-forth conversation between two characters. Nehemiah supplemented the account of this dialogue by candidly inserting his emotional responses. In doing so, he intensified the pall of sadness hang-ing over the entire scene. Let's examine how the conversation unfolds.

Read Nehemiah 2:1–2.

Nehemiah's distress caught King Artaxerxes's attention. The king's observant question about his cupbearer's obvious sorrow passed through Nehemiah's heart like a dagger. Gene Getz explains why Nehemiah reacted with such fear:

> A servant was never to let his negative emotions show before the king, for it might suggest dissatisfaction with the king. To do so might jeopardize his position or even his life.[2]

In light of this, and with the knowledge that Artaxerxes had already prevented previous attempts at reconstruction, Nehemiah chose his next words carefully—and prayerfully.

 Read Nehemiah 2:3–4.

It's as though a dam was beginning to crumble in the king's heart, with channels of water rushing around it. The cupbearer recognized who was at work—the God of heaven softened the heart of the king of earth.

In Nehemiah 2:2–4, what is significant about how Nehemiah responded to his fear during his interchange with the king?

_____

_____

_____

What does this reveal about Nehemiah's view of God? Of prayer?

_____

Read Nehemiah 2:5–6.

The king's questions reflect a deep appreciation for Nehemiah and his service, and he wanted his cupbearer to come back. This tells us something important about Nehemiah. Although his heart longed for Jerusalem, he had obviously carried out his important, self-sacrificing duties in this foreign land with the same care he would have given them in his homeland. And the words tacked on the end of Nehemiah's request, "and I gave him a definite time," reveal an important leadership quality: the importance of planning and organization. Nehemiah's well-thought-out itinerary was the result of four months of prayerfully planning the whole project while waiting on God to move Artaxerxes's heart according to His own sovereign timing. Stepping out in faith doesn't imply acting haphazardly or launching out foolishly. In planning and prayer, dependence and action, God's sovereignty and our responsibility work in harmony.

 DIGGING DEEPER
Sovereignty vs. Responsibility

God's sovereignty and human responsibility tug at each other in theological tension. Is God sovereign? Yes. Are people responsible to act? Yes. We can stretch this tension between divine sovereignty and human responsibility to its breaking point if we try to fully comprehend the power of prayer as it relates to God's predetermined plan.

We know that in His sovereign plan, God works out all things for our good (Romans 8:28), and yet He always responds to our prayers (1 John 5:14–15). How can that be? Scripture presents a great variety of prayers that were answered, often in ways that surprise us. God answered Paul's reasonable prayer for freedom from his "thorn in the flesh" with a clear "no" (2 Corinthians 12:7–10). He chose to answer the misguided petition of the Israelites for a king "like the nations" according to their will, even though the answer involved negative consequences (1 Samuel 8:19–22). In the case of Solomon, God answered his prayer for wisdom, and then added blessings for which he didn't even ask (2 Chronicles 1:11–12). In short, in concert with our prayers, God works in various ways to bring about His perfect will as well as our ultimate good.

How, exactly, do our own wills, responses, and choices harmonize with God's sovereign will and infinite knowledge? We may never understand such a profound mystery, but we can still respond to this mystery by obeying Scripture's admonitions to do our part in seeking the Lord in prayer and giving Him the glory for what He accomplishes in, through, and often in spite of us!

According to Ephesians 6:5–9 and Colossians 3:22–4:1, what are the responsibilities of both an employee and an employer?

Employee ("servant")   Employer ("master")

_____   _____

_____   _____

_____   _____

_____   _____

_____   _____

How did Nehemiah reflect this in his relationship to Artaxerxes?

_____

_____

We know Nehemiah waited about four months from the time he received the news concerning Jerusalem to when he finally discussed the matter with the king. Based on the account thus far, how do you think Nehemiah discerned the proper timing for this crucial conversation?

_____

_____

_____

_____

In the few minutes it took for the conversation in Nehemiah 2:2–6 to transpire, Nehemiah switched roles from cupbearer to builder. He immediately got to work, respectfully requesting from King Artaxerxes what he already knew he would need.

 Read Nehemiah 2:7–8.

Because God had directed the desires of the king's heart to flow in the same direction as Nehemiah's, the king was pleased to provide what his faithful servant needed. As the curtain closes on this scene, Nehemiah's words bring us back to the truth of Proverbs 21:1 and to the real reason behind his success: "The good hand of my God was on me" (Nehemiah 2:8).

NEHEMIAH EN ROUTE

In a brief interlude before the final scene concludes this lesson, the setting of Nehemiah's chronicle moves more than eight hundred miles. With the king's letters and a royal escort, Nehemiah had no trouble securing passage through the gates of distant provinces (Nehemiah 2:9). God had provided far more than Nehemiah needed! He had letters from the king, officers and horsemen, resources for his journey, and even the means to procure timber for his own house! What a thrill it must have been for Nehemiah to recognize God at work as he followed His lead. But verse 10 reveals a hint of opposition in the form of two antagonists, Sanballat the Horonite and Tobiah the Ammonite.

 Read Nehemiah 2:9–11.

For many people, an encounter with opposition immediately raises doubt about whether or not they're really following God's will. In Nehemiah's case, however, the opposition of those who despised the things of God served as an affirmation that he *was* doing God's will. In lesson 5, we will examine more closely how Nehemiah faced the opposition of outsiders.

Nehemiah spent four months fervently praying and waiting, then risked his life before Artaxerxes and journeyed more than eight hundred miles through hostile lands. Finally, he passed along the rugged ridge leading up to Jerusalem. There, from a distance, he surveyed the rubble he would some-how transform into the rebuilt wall of Jerusalem. God's builder had arrived, but no one knew it . . . yet.

STARTING YOUR JOURNEY

 Whether the setting was Artaxerxes's opulent palace in Susa or the run-down city of Jerusalem, Nehemiah's story points us toward an important truth about effective leadership: in addi-tion to prayer, preparation is essential. Nehemiah's preparation offers no less than four key principles for those who seek to follow God's will, especially when they serve under difficult bosses.

First, *changing the heart is God's specialty*. No matter how important the person, God is the one who decides if, how, and when someone's heart will bend. He may use a variety of means and circumstances, but if God wills it, we can count on it.

Second, *prayer and waiting go hand in hand.* You haven't really prayed until you've learned to abandon your own efforts at manipulation and to wait on God to work in His timing.

Third, *faith is not a synonym for disorder or a substitute for a well-thought-out plan.* God honors and expects careful thinking and planning from His children. We are to use the brains He's given us! Although we can embrace the truth that "God causes all things to work together for good to those who love God" (Romans 8:28), "all things" also includes our careful planning and faithful execution of those plans.

Fourth, *opposition often reinforces the will of God rather than hinders it.* When we walk in His footsteps we can expect to encounter some Sanballats and Tobiahs who oppose us along the way. This may affirm, rather than refute, that we're exactly where we need to be.

As you consider any difficult people in leadership over you (boss, teacher, parent, or husband), can you identify a particular manipulative technique you use—the silent treatment, flattery, or sarcasm—that you need to replace with prayer? If so, what is it?

_____

_____

Read Matthew 5:43–47 and Luke 6:27–36. What prevents you from turning this person over to the power of God right now?

_____

_____

Could it be that you are the "problem person" for someone else? How would you want that person to communicate this to you?

_____

_____

_____

Of the four principles on page 32–33, which best applies to your present situation? What can you do specifically to apply this principle in your words or actions this week?

_____

_____

_____

_____

Problem projects and problem people stand within the jurisdiction of our sovereign God. He can soften the hardest heart in answer to the prayers of His saints. When He does, we must be ready and willing to act, to step forward in faith, to begin to accomplish what the Lord set before us, regardless of the opposition. Wise leaders know that prayer for God's actions and preparation for our own actions go hand-in-hand.

LESSON FOUR

Getting off Dead Center

Nehemiah 2:11–20

 THE HEART OF THE MATTER

When Nehemiah journeyed to Jerusalem to rebuild the wall, he faced the immense task of inspiring those around him to pick up bricks and begin a grueling project. Some were young novices with soft, callous-free hands. Others were old and accustomed to living without the wall—perhaps lethargic and disinterested. The sands of time had smothered much of the patriotic zeal that had once burned in the hearts of the Jews. It's easy to see that motivating them would be one of Nehemiah's first challenges of leadership. In this lesson we'll learn the technique he employed to motivate them to rise up and begin a massive project.

 DISCOVERING THE WAY

Two kindred years, 444 BC and AD 1940. Two significant leaders . . . called out in different centuries to similar crises.

In BC Jerusalem, the city walls lay in ruins and the gates had been burned. In AD London, the walls of homes, businesses, and churches had collapsed, and columns of smoke rose to blacken the sky. In Jerusalem, the people suffered great distress and reproach from their enemies. In London, a malaise of despair and sorrow weakened the hearts of the people as a ruthless tyrant from Germany ravaged Europe, gobbling up entire nations. Now the jaws of his war machine were closing in on Great Britain.

The leader who rebuilt the walls of Jerusalem was, of course, Nehemiah. And the man who led the British out of Hitler's maelstrom of destruction was Winston Churchill. Like an army, the words of his stirring speeches fought their way into the hearts of the people and routed the fear that held them captive. United behind the "Bulldog of Britain," the British became a tenacious and fierce force whose power the Nazis had underestimated.

As a leader, Churchill faced many of the same challenges Nehemiah did. The Prime Minister's words directed to President Roosevelt—"Give us the tools, and we will finish the job"[1]—remind us of Nehemiah's request to King Artaxerxes—to paraphrase, "Give me permission to build, timber to build with, and safe passage past my enemies, and we'll finish the job" (Nehemiah 2:7–8).

And both men finished the job. They led their people from near defeat to absolute victory with the same bulldogged determination and ability to motivate found in all great leaders.

What means of motivation have you seen leaders use to get results?

_____

_____

_____

_____

In your realms of leadership, what methods of motivation seem to work best? Why?

_____

_____

_____

What tends to demotivate the people under your leadership?

_____

_____

_____

_____

Did you find it difficult to answer these questions? Why?

_____

_____

PRIVATE INVESTIGATION OF THE SCENE

Nehemiah described his arrival in Jerusalem in the first half of Nehemiah 2:11: "So I came to Jerusalem." He then dropped out of sight in the next phrase: "and was there three days." Three days without a word to anyone. No luncheons with city officials, no press conferences, no guided tours around the wall, no fireworks or parade down Main Street. Only silence.

The reason for Nehemiah's baffling behavior comes to light in verses 12 and 16. While he avoided public attention for three days, Nehemiah was meeting with an important official, the real "Mayor of Jerusalem," Yahweh. He took a private tour of the walls—at night, without sharing his purpose publicly.

Read Nehemiah 2:12, 16.

After arriving in Jerusalem, Nehemiah's first order of business was to seek silence and solitude for the purpose of undisturbed reflection. During those first three quiet days, Nehemiah paused to learn. He purposefully avoided the crowds and the political fanfare that would have undoubtedly accompanied a leader with the authority of King Artaxerxes. Nehemiah concerned himself with the task itself—without the pressure of public opinion. Great leaders exhibit this same character trait of pausing to learn, to gather information, to size up the job with their own eyes.

Before launching into challenging tasks, other great leaders in Scripture made a habit of seeking God in silence and solitude. Moses spent forty years in the desert of Midian (see Acts 7:29–30) before God used him to lead His people out of Egypt (Exodus 2:15; 4:19). The apostle Paul began his earth-shaking missionary work in a place we know only as Arabia (Galatians 1:17–18). In three years away from the public eye, he was transformed from a fastidious Pharisee into a devoted disciple of Christ. And the One you would least expect to need time alone with God was the One who enjoyed perfect fellowship with Him at all times. The Lord Jesus hungered for special times of intimacy with His Father spent in silence and solitude away from the crowds (Matthew 14:13, 23; Mark 1:35–37; 6:30–32; Luke 6:12–13).

Imagine you are one of the many men or women who followed Christ and His disciples during their itinerant preaching. Give three good reasons why some might think that Jesus's times away from the crowds would be a waste of valuable ministry time.

What are your own reasons for neglecting times of silence and solitude with God?

_____

_____

_____

_____

During World War II, Churchill remained intimately aware of the realities at "ground zero" by visiting areas that had been damaged by the German blitzkrieg, encouraging victims, and inspecting defenses. Similarly, Nehemiah immediately set about inspecting Jerusalem's main defense, the wall, and gathering firsthand information about the damage inflicted by the Babylonian "blitz."

 Read Nehemiah 2:13–15.

NEHEMIAH'S JERUSALEM

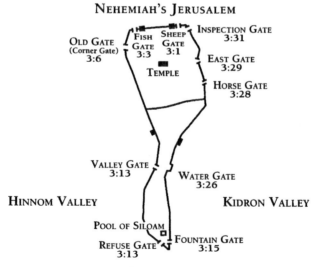

Like an investigator bent on solving a crime or a physician preparing to conduct a life-changing procedure, Nehemiah the builder carefully examined the situation. He probed his way around the wall's gaping holes, even dismounting and trekking on foot. He had to gather facts, make plans, and prepare to delegate as he readied himself for a critical challenge that every leader faces: motivating others.

Companies and organizations often call upon motivational speakers to inspire their employees or members to greater productivity or positive attitudes. But these high-powered pep talks miss the mark in one important way—the speaker rarely knows the *reality* of the circumstances—the actual day-in, day-out problems and concerns of the people as they work on their projects. Nehemiah knew that motivation means more than just positive words fired indiscriminately into a crowd. Motivation begins by intimately understanding the task. One famous author on leadership quipped, "Being an effective department supervisor on a manufacturing floor is fundamentally different from giving seminars about it."[2]

Are you familiar enough with the everyday struggles of those you lead to give them more than just a surface-level pep talk? Test yourself by summarizing the top three everyday challenges of those working under your realms of leadership.

_____

_____

_____

_____

What can you do to better relate to the struggles of those who look to you for leadership and motivation? What is your equivalent to examining the walls like Nehemiah or visiting the wounded like Churchill?

_____

_____

_____

OPEN DISCUSSION OF THE NEED

With the opening phrase of Nehemiah 2:17, Nehemiah left the harbor of silence and solitude and launched into the sea of the public eye. Now we hear the well-informed speech Nehemiah used for recruiting.

 Read Nehemiah 2:17–18.

Winston Churchill's first statement as Prime Minister to the House of Commons during World War II was, "I have nothing to offer but blood, toil, tears and sweat."[3] With those words, Churchill laid aside all the encumbrances of British protocol and got down to the serious business of committing himself to the people and their most pressing need—protection of their homeland. In Nehemiah's first address as God's leader for rebuilding the wall, he too identified with the people and committed himself to the task of helping to protect their homeland.

In Nehemiah 2:17, note the pronouns "we" and "us." What does this type of language communicate to those under a person's leadership?

_____

_____

_____

How might this attitude help to motivate people who feel burned-out and in need of encouragement? What actions need to accompany these words in order for them to be taken seriously?

_____

_____

_____

Nehemiah laid to rest any doubts about whether he was just some prattling official with papers from Persia or a genuine brother who shared the distress and reproach of the Jews. The people were motivated by Nehemiah's sincere offer of "blood, toil, tears, and sweat" to rebuild the city's protective wall.

Besides this, Nehemiah laid out the hard facts about the dire situation. He was honest and straightforward. And he made no effort to motivate the people with external rewards or gimmicks like new chariots, campouts at the Dead Sea, or bricks with their names on them in the wall. Though workers need to be adequately compensated, strictly material incentives produce short-lived enthusiasm and lead to feelings of entitlement. Enduring motivation is that which comes from within—intrinsic motivation that appeals to their immaterial, spiritual desires. Nehemiah appealed to the Jews' desire to do what God wanted them to do—to assume national prominence again as God's holy people.

By pointing to the ways God had already begun the work, Nehemiah instilled hope and faith in the people. God was up to something big— greater than any one individual, family, or tribe—and they could become a part of it. "So," Nehemiah wrote, "they put their hands to the good work" (Nehemiah 2:18).

In your experience, how well have extrinsic or external, material motivators worked in your realms of leadership?

_____

_____

_____

Have you been able to tap into intrinsic, internal, personal, and immaterial motivations among your people? Why do you think this type is generally more effective? How might you improve on this type of motivation?

_____

_____

_____

Why is it important for the leader to have the same type of motivation?

_____

_____

_____

DIRECT CRITICISM OF THE PLAN

In an address given on December 30, 1941, over a year after the beginning of Germany's occupation of France, Churchill recalled how the British were mocked for their decision to stand and fight:

> When I warned [the French] that Britain would fight on alone whatever they did, their generals told their prime minister and his divided cabinet, "In three weeks England will have her neck wrung like a chicken." Some chicken; some neck.[4]

No sooner had Nehemiah convinced the Israelites to stand and rebuild than they encountered some of the same kinds of ridicule and mocking. But Nehemiah stood his ground against the verbal volleys and put the reputation of the promise-keeping God of Israel on the line.

 Read Nehemiah 2:19–20.

Like Nehemiah's stand millennia earlier, the Bulldog of Britain once said to Hitler in defiance, "We will have no truce or parley with you [Hitler], or the grisly gang who work your wicked will. You do your worst—and we will do our best."[5] A commitment to do what's right goes far to fuel the passions of the righteous.

How do you think Nehemiah's strong words against Sanballat, Tobiah, and Geshem helped motivate his people? What source of power was he relying on?

_____

_____

_____

STARTING YOUR JOURNEY

Nehemiah and Churchill—at times it is difficult to tell these great leaders apart; their styles of leadership and motivation were so successful. Nehemiah devoted his iron constitution and inexhaustible energy to the salvation of Israel and to the values Israel stood for in a pagan world. But most importantly, he focused his total concentration on the Lord in every circumstance:

Alone: in deliberate *solitude*

"I did not tell anyone what my God was putting into my mind to do for Jerusalem" (Nehemiah 2:12).

In Public: among his people with *motivational words*

"I told them how the hand of my God had been favorable to me" (2:18).

Under Attack: before his enemies with *sharp rebukes*

"The God of heaven will give us success" (2:20).

After observing each of these three elements of a godly leader's spiritual focus, which do you feel is most lacking in your current realms of leadership?

_____

For the element you chose, write out a plan for this week that will allow you to take a concrete, credible step toward strengthening one of the following:

1. Your time of solitude to better familiarize yourself with the people and projects you're called to oversee
2. Your words of genuine encouragement and motivation both to individuals and to groups
3. Your decisive rebukes against obvious demotivators who threaten the stability of your people

_____

_____

_____

Motivating people to do the day-in, day-out menial tasks is hard enough. Motivating them to do difficult tasks in the face of stiff opposition can seem impossible. Wrapped in a warm blanket of prayer, a leader must stay aware of the needs of the people and the details of the project while remaining wise in his or her words of encouragement. This takes conscious effort and reflective solitude followed by words and actions that ignite internal motivation. Remember, though, only God changes hearts and motivates people to do great things.

LESSON FIVE

Knocked Down, but Not Knocked Out

Nehemiah 4:1–9

 THE HEART OF THE MATTER

As soon as Nehemiah and his crew began to rebuild the walls of Jerusalem (Nehemiah 3), opposition and criticism broke out and constantly bombarded them from all sides. In this lesson, we will discover how a leader should handle the inevitable and unavoidable criticism that comes from the outside. Nehemiah's example teaches us that it is possible not only to stay at our task regardless of the opposition, but also to do it in a way that deepens our walk with God. Criticism may knock us down, but it doesn't have to knock us out!

DISCOVERING THE WAY

J. Oswald Sanders, in his biblical and practical book *Spiritual Leadership*, wrote, "No leader is exempt from criticism, and his humility will nowhere be seen more clearly than in the manner in which he accepts and reacts to it."[1]

All criticism, however, is not equal. *Constructive* criticism comes from genuine partners in or supporters of a leader's work. Positive critics are motivated by a desire to help, not hinder, the leader. Therefore they share their concerns in a humble, respectful way. Godly leaders learn to seek out constructive criticism from wise mentors and fellow workers. And they seek to apply their wisdom judiciously. Every leader will also quickly become familiar with *destructive* criticism that is designed to tear down, discredit, and malign.

Who are your most trusted constructive critics?

_____

_____

Concisely describe their mannerisms, methods, and motives as they share constructive criticism.

_____

_____

_____

How do you generally respond to this kind of criticism?

_____

_____

_____

As our study of Nehemiah continues, our hero will come face to face with destructive criticism. But first, let's glance at a New Testament character known for his firsthand experience with opposition.

A NEW TESTAMENT PERSPECTIVE

Of all the New Testament books Paul wrote, 2 Corinthians is one of the most autobiographical. In it Paul provided some honest admissions about ministry. Consider his words in chapter 4: "But we have this treasure in earthen vessels, that the surpassing greatness of the power may be of God and not from ourselves" (4:7). Paul admitted his human frailty. He recognized that his ministry's power did not come from himself but from the Lord. He went on to describe what the life of an earthen vessel is like.

> We are afflicted in every way, but not crushed; perplexed, but not despairing; persecuted, but not forsaken; struck down, but not destroyed; always carrying about in the body the dying of Jesus, that the life of Jesus also may be manifested in our body.
> (2 Corinthians 4:8–10)

Did you notice that all-inclusive word which begins verse 10? "*Always* carrying about . . ." (emphasis added). The marks of Jesus's death are obvious in the lives of the people God uses most. Why? "That the life of Jesus also may be manifested in our body" (4:10).

God is not only interested in blessing a humble "clay pot," He is also interested in using the vessel itself as an object lesson in godliness. He puts the truth in a human life and then places that life in front of an audience, whether it's a Bible-study group of five or a professional corporation of five thousand. He uses regular individuals to *display*, not just hold, the glory of God.

Paul's words in verses 8–10 contain an implicit promise . . . but not the kind we like to hear: opposition is inevitable. And yet to counter the discouragement that follows such a promise comes radiant, God-given hope: We may be knocked down, but we're not knocked out!

In your current realms of leadership, who are your toughest destructive critics or opponents?

_____

_____

Describe their mannerisms, methods, and motives when they offer criticism.

_____

_____

_____

How have you handled their attacks in the past? By avoiding, ignoring, defending, or fighting back? Why do you think you tend to respond in this way?

_____

_____

_____

THE OLD TESTAMENT EXAMPLE OF NEHEMIAH

When we left Nehemiah, he was just getting ready to start rebuilding the wall around Jerusalem (Nehemiah 2:20). As we join him now, he's already in the thick of the work (4:1). We've skipped over Nehemiah 3, in which Nehemiah appointed various workmen for different parts of the job. That chapter illustrates that Nehemiah was keenly interested in *people*, not just projects—painting a more complete picture of Nehemiah's character. The action of the chronicle picks up again in Nehemiah 4, and so shall we.

As we have seen, rebuilding the wall had gotten off to a good start. Nehemiah's boss, King Artaxerxes, had not only given him time off to oversee the project but also provided some needed materials and secured

Nehemiah's safe passage to Jerusalem. Even the people of Jerusalem willingly came alongside Nehemiah and began working diligently, and they faced only a few hints of opposition (Nehemiah 2:10, 19) . . .

. . . Until now.

Enter again Sanballat and Tobiah: critics extraordinaire. As the wall grew daily, their irritation escalated.

 Read Nehemiah 4:1–3.

Sanballat and Tobiah's dialogue sounded more like that of junior high kids sitting on the sidelines snickering at another school's football team than the words of powerful leaders. One might expect that a small band of Jews valiantly undertaking such an overwhelming task would inspire respect and applause . . . or at least pity. But not in these men. The signs of progress and growth incited them to sarcastic opposition. Like most habitual critics, they felt threatened by the thought of change and saw it as something to be resisted. Also, like most critics, they looked at the situation from only their human point of view— they didn't take God's ultimate plan into consideration.

Did you notice something else about the conversation in 4:1–3? It was *one-sided*; it did not contain one ounce of balanced perspective. One man's comments incited similar comments from another. Critics often associate with other critics. They like to be around people who will reinforce their views. In the case of Sanballat, he chose to run with Tobiah and another naysayer named Geshem (we'll hear more from him in Nehemiah 6:1). They were close friends at least in part because of their mutual love of destructive criticism.

What types of critical comments are the most difficult for you to hear? Give a few recent examples.

_____

_____

_____

What is it about these remarks that makes them linger in your mind?

_____

_____

_____

Every group—including every church or ministry—has its Sanballats and Tobiahs. They are unavoidable. So how do we handle them? Let's look at Nehemiah's response to negative, destructive criticism.

Often our first reaction to criticism is a quick retort. But Nehemiah kept his cool. _His first response was to talk to God._

Read Nehemiah 4:4–5.

We can tell from Nehemiah's requests that he felt like retaliating. Wouldn't you? But instead of striking back, he spent some therapeutic time on his knees, bringing his concerns before God. It takes two to argue, but an argument dies on the spot if one person refuses to participate. And it's the words that fly thoughtlessly off our tongues that we regret later, not the ones that have been pondered in secret before the Lord.

Read Proverbs 15:1, 28. Practically speaking, how did Nehemiah's response illustrate the principles found in these verses?

_____

_____

Notice a second thing about Nehemiah's response to Sanballat's criticism—*he stayed at the task.*

 Read Nehemiah 4:6.

Critics demoralize; leaders encourage. We know from Nehemiah 4:5 that Sanballat's barbs had pricked a hole in the people's enthusiasm, but Nehemiah kept them focused on the task and encouraged them to work with renewed determination. We can imagine him standing up after his time of prayer and shouting, "Keep pouring that mortar! Bring on those stones! Keep going, and God's going to help us build this wall!"

Nothing riles critics more than having their criticism result in further progress. The sight of those Jews slathering on that mortar and hauling in those stones made Sanballat and his cohorts more furious than ever. So, instead of backing off, they strengthened their attack.

DOORWAY TO HISTORY
Money, Money, Money

Have you ever wondered why Sanballat and the wealthy men of Samaria so vigorously opposed Nehemiah's work? The answer is simple: *money.*

One commentator noted:

> Put bluntly, "a powerful Jerusalem means a depressed Samaria." One of the main highways linking the

Tigris-Euphrates river valley to the north with Egypt in the south and Philistia to the west passes through Jerusalem. With Jerusalem once more a well-protected city, its very location [would] attract trade; and gone [would] be Samaria's economic supremacy in "the land beyond the river."[2]

Not much has changed, has it? In today's world of business, academics, politics—and sad to say even ministry—economics is what motivates much of the opposition, positioning, and fighting. Because every endeavor depends on the availability of finances, discouragement can easily turn to pressure, stress, and strain and give rise to all kinds of arguments and backbiting.

 Read Nehemiah 4:7–9.

Though the critics conspired to unleash a full-blown frontal assault, Nehemiah wouldn't stand for defeat. Yet for all his determination, he didn't try to take matters into his own hands. He matched intensified opposition with intensified prayer, this time bringing his workers with him to the throne of God (Nehemiah 4:9).

Nehemiah thought practically as well as prudently. He brought his frustration to God, and he also took action. When you know a robber is in the neighborhood, you lock your doors tightly. And when you know your enemy doesn't like your wall, you guard it carefully.

What steps have you taken to shield yourself and those who depend on your leadership from the painful effects of destructive criticism? If you have not done anything, consider what steps you should take.

_____

_____

_____

_____

 STARTING YOUR JOURNEY

No one has ever been able to completely avoid criticism. Yes, it can be demoralizing, discouraging, and incite us to do or say things we later regret. We've all been there, and we will be again. But what worked in Nehemiah's situation centuries ago can work just as well in our lives today.

First, *realize that it is impossible to lead without facing criticism.* Whether you're the CEO of a Fortune 500 company or the president of the PTA, if you lead you will hear complaints from jealous and jeering outsiders or competitors. You can count on it. And if you don't actually hear them, you might as well assume somebody is criticizing in private. So refuse to view criticism as a sign of failure; recognize it as a part of the fallen world we live in.

Second, *it is essential that your first response to opposition is prayer.* There's no better place to cool your anger and gain perspective on your actions than on your knees. Once again, Nehemiah illustrated this principle well.

Third, *prayer may not be all that is necessary if opposition intensifies.* If you notice a fire blazing in your kitchen, you need to pray for God to save you, but you also need to start spraying some water! God gave us minds and bodies so that we may take practical action when it's needed. Prayer should always be the preface to action.

When it comes right down to it, the barbs of carping critics and pesky pessimists are usually not worth the worry they cause. Every project and leader has its adversaries. When appropriate, listen to their comments to determine if what they have to say has any validity. But if you detect the singsong ring of a lifelong naysayer, follow Nehemiah's example. Don't let it rattle you, and don't let it hinder the work God has given you to do. Criticism may knock you down, but don't let it knock you out!

If you're being harangued by criticism, take some time to think through the following questions.

How does this particular criticism make you feel? Hurt, angry, or frightened? What does the Bible say about how to deal with these emotions? (To find specific verses, you may wish to consult a Bible concordance. One can be found online, at a library, or often in the back of your Bible.)

What major or minor issues does the criticism really focus on? Are these legitimate concerns? Why, or why not?

Do you perceive that ulterior motives might be driving the critic, such as pride, jealousy, cynicism, stubbornness, or greed? If so, should you change your response?

_____

_____

_____

After pondering these questions thoroughly, address each one with God in prayer. With Nehemiah's example in mind, formulate a wise, appropriate response to the criticism you face—a response that will keep you focused on the leadership task God has called you to complete.

_____

_____

_____

Leaders will face criticism. It is inevitable and unavoidable. While we can learn from constructive criticism, destructive criticism can be demoralizing, debilitating, and distracting. But through prayer and a wise response, we can keep the task in front of us and our people with us. Has criticism knocked you to the ground? While you're there, spend time with God in prayer, and then get up and go. As it does to all leaders, criticism will occasionally knock you down . . . but it doesn't have to knock you out.

LESSON SIX

Discouragement: Its Causes and Cure

Nehemiah 4:9–23

 THE HEART OF THE MATTER

The further we travel through the pages of Nehemiah, the more we discover the value and relevance of its instruction for every level of leadership. As we turn to Nehemiah 4:9–23, we find Nehemiah's work crew discouraged for the first time since the project of rebuilding the walls around Jerusalem began. But what caused the discouragement? And how did Nehemiah solve this problem? The answers to these questions apply directly to the discouragement many leaders face today.

 DISCOVERING THE WAY

A mother of eight children came home one day to find her five youngest huddled intently in the middle of the floor. She walked over to see what the center of attraction was and discovered they were playing with five baby skunks. Panic-stricken, she shouted, "Run, children, run!" And run they did—each clutching one terrified skunk![1]

Can you imagine five kids with skunks, all running in different directions? The farther the children run, the louder the mother shouts, causing all five to panic and squeeze their skunks . . . and skunks don't like to be squeezed!

We've all had a problem blow up in our face and end up as a stinking mess. Those situations can knock the wind right out of our confidence and leave us feeling flat and discouraged. Nehemiah discovered this when his seemingly simple task turned into a sizable problem. He set out to build a wall, but his people soon began to struggle with criticism from outside and frustration from within. They became discouraged, and their work suffered.

What tends to discourage you the most? Reflect on a time or two when you've experienced discouragement. What factors were involved? Were they mostly task-oriented or people-oriented?

_____

_____

_____

_____

In the past, how have you tried to prevent or resolve discouragement? Have your methods been effective? Why, or why not?

_____

_____

_____

_____

THE CAUSES OF DISCOURAGEMENT

As we observed in the last lesson, while Nehemiah's workers were building up Jerusalem's broken walls a little more each day, their confidence and faith were being torn down, brick by brick. The repeated threats and criticism from their enemies chiseled away at their resolve and determination (Nehemiah 4:5). And in spite of Nehemiah's efforts to encourage the people, discouragement finally brought their work to a standstill. Let's take a closer look at the problem and see what caused the discouragement and how Nehemiah dealt with it.

 Read Nehemiah 4:10–12.

The Contemporary English Version of the Bible renders the lament in verse 10, "So much rubble for us to haul! / Worn out and weary, / will we ever finish this wall?" *The Message* adds in verse 10: "The builders are pooped!" We can imagine the tired workers throwing their hands up and heaving a collective sigh.

The first source of the Israelites' discouragement was a *loss of strength.* The people were burned-out physically. They were stumbling, tottering, staggering under the load. One of the main reasons for rebuilding the wall was for the protection it would provide. But in their haste, the people neglected to protect themselves from the enemy within—exhaustion. They started strong, but they were too tired to finish.

Another source of discouragement was their *loss of vision.* The Hebrew word for "rubbish" in Nehemiah 4:10 means "dry earth, debris."[2] The people were tired; they had worked hard. But instead of being encouraged by what they had already accomplished, they saw only the huge task before them—all the "rubbish" that needed to be cleaned up. They couldn't imagine the end goal: a completed wall.

A third source of discouragement was their *loss of confidence.* The erosion of the people's physical reserves and vision also affected their confidence. At one time the people "had a mind to work" (Nehemiah 4:6). Now, their motivation had vanished, and in its place loomed an overwhelming feeling that they could never finish the task that they had so joyfully begun.

Finally, the Jews felt a *loss of security*. They faced vocal and violent enemies who didn't want to see them succeed (Nehemiah 4:11). The people had to place each brick while looking over their shoulders, not knowing from moment to moment whether they might be attacked and their work destroyed.

In your own realms of leadership, have the following sources of discouragement ever affected either you or those serving with you? In what ways?

Loss of strength

_____

_____

Loss of vision

_____

_____

Loss of confidence

_____

_____

Loss of security

_____

_____

Which of these is the most potent source of discouragement for you? Why?

_____

_____

_____

NEHEMIAH'S CURE FOR DISCOURAGEMENT

Nehemiah must have felt somewhat like that mother with the baby skunks—out of control and with a mess on his hands. The troops were wilting with discouragement, and his project was crumbling before his eyes. But Nehemiah didn't stand around wringing his hands. Instead, he put five specific steps into action in order to rebuild the people's confidence.

 Read Nehemiah 4:13–23.

First, *Nehemiah unified the people around the same goal* (Nehemiah 4:13). Nehemiah noticed that the basic unit of encouragement, the family, had been broken because relatives worked at different places on the walls. Scattering the work was also counterproductive; they could have accomplished far more by working as a team. So he reorganized the work and placed his people into family units centered around common goals.

Second, *Nehemiah directed the people's attention to the Lord* (Nehemiah 4:14). Nehemiah saw his people's fear and knew that he must point them back to the Lord. Unless they changed their focus from their obstacles to their goal, they would make very little progress.

Third, *Nehemiah encouraged the people to maintain a balance* (Nehemiah 4:15–17). Some workers probably wanted to concentrate on building the protective wall. Others wanted to grab their spears and go to war. Nehemiah brought about balance by directing them to continue the work while also being prepared to fight.

Fourth, *Nehemiah provided a rallying point for the people* (Nehemiah 4:18–20). Nehemiah's rallying point involved a *place*. He knew the enemy could attack at any time, in any place. The people needed to know that if one section of the wall was put under siege, others would drop what they were doing and rally to their aid at that location. The rallying point also involved a *principle*: mutual encouragement. Nehemiah bolstered his people's faith by reminding them that their fellow Israelites as well as their God would be fighting alongside them. They would not be left to fight alone.

Fifth, *Nehemiah occupied the people with service to others* (Nehemiah 4:21–23). Nehemiah created a protective "buddy system." He knew that if the people were involved in serving one another regularly and consistently, strong relationships would form, and their confidence and morale about the work at hand would increase.

OUR RESPONSE TODAY

Regardless of the task—a project at work, a challenging ministry situation, or a challenging aspect of our Christian lives—many of us start out with confidence but soon find ourselves deeply discouraged through loss of strength, vision, confidence, or security. Whether we're halfway through constructing a wall or half-finished with paying off a debt, discouragement may catch us unaware. It tends to pull the focus of our hearts and minds onto ourselves. It can quell our hunger for knowing and trusting in Christ and lead us to trust in our own feeble abilities. But don't let discouragement take hold! Follow Nehemiah's guidelines for encouragement, and resume your task with a renewed spirit.

STARTING YOUR JOURNEY

In the seasons of leadership, you'll experience times when those you lead feel discouraged. The result? Bad morale that spreads like a disease, low productivity that affects the bottom line, a lack of creativity and new ideas, and ultimately a mass exodus or high turnover rate. If you've been through these periods of discouragement recently, chances are your heart is pounding at the thought.

But you can resolve, and even prevent, discouragement from overtaking you and those under your leadership. Nehemiah put an end to discouragement among his workers by five means. As you think through these biblical methods for dealing with discouragement, consider your current realm of leadership and the presence or absence of these principles.

First, *unify people around the same goal.* Remind people of the major purpose of the organization, ministry, or family and of each person's or group's role in achieving that purpose. This may also require strategic reorganization to help move people in a common, unified direction.

What are the primary goals of your realms of leadership? Do you feel that you and those who serve with you are focused on those goals? If not, how could you create a renewed focus on your goals?

_____

_____

_____

_____

_____

Then, *direct their attention to the Lord.* During times of discouragement, it's important for us to refocus our attention on the Lord. Meditate on His promises, memorize His Word, and reflect on His character.

Do you spend time in prayer, Bible study, or reading Scripture with those under your leadership? How might you incorporate those things into your time together?

_____

_____

_____

Next, *encourage them to maintain a balance.* When we're discouraged, it's easy to get caught in the swing of an emotional pendulum—to see only one perspective at a time, never the whole picture. Maintaining balance helps keep people focused on the Lord and on the overall goal of the organization, group, or project.

Consider the competing issues that vie for attention in your realms of leadership—finances, personnel issues, deadlines, and so on. Do you feel that these issues are handled in a balanced manner, or does one dominate over the others? If one is receiving too much attention, what can you do to regain a balanced perspective? Be specific.

_____

_____

_____

_____

Provide a rallying point. Every individual and team needs a rallying point—a mental rendezvous when trouble or attack from the enemy comes. If we delay, hesitate, or dawdle in the face of crises, discouragement will set in. In light of potential terrorist threats and natural disasters, many families and organizations have come up with an "emergency management plan." Similarly, designing an "encouragement plan" in case of crisis will help leaders deal with potential discouragement quickly and effectively. People need to know they are not alone in what they are facing. Incorporate a physical place, mental focus, and emotional emphasis to facilitate interaction and encouragement.

Take a few moments to sketch out an "encouragement plan" for your realms of leadership. What physical, mental, and emotional elements might you include? Also, remember that in order for those under your leadership to have strong ties in times of crisis, relationships must be cultivated and established along the way.

_____

_____

_____

_____

_____

_____

Is there a person within your group who seems to be a natural encourager—someone who is well-respected by others, who exhibits a positive attitude and a genuine concern for others? How might you draw on his or her strengths as you implement your plan?

_____

_____

_____

Finally, *occupy them with serving each other*. If our investment in each other's lives comes only during times of crisis, our interpersonal relationships will not withstand the storms of discouragement. However, when people consistently show they value each other beyond their tasks by actively serving one another, morale will be high, relationships will be strong, and discouragement will be rare. When the storms of discouragement move in on such strong relationships, they will often break like waves against rocks.

How might you encourage those in your realms of leadership to serve one another? List several specific tasks you might assign, emphases you might make, or opportunities you might provide. Then, commit to following through with at least one of your ideas.

_____

_____

_____

_____

_____

_____

Though they were at one time enthusiastic and energetic, Nehemiah's workers grew weary and discouraged. They lost their strength, vision, confidence, and security. But Nehemiah, overcoming his own discouragement, took up the task of curing their melancholy mood through a variety of God-directed means. During times of discouragement, it's important for us to refocus our attention on the Lord and on the goal, to maintain a healthy balance, to return to a rallying point, and to reenergize our spirits through ministry to others.

LESSON SEVEN

Love, Loans . . . and the Money Crunch

Nehemiah 5:1–13

THE HEART OF THE MATTER

Every worthy task contains its share of challenges. And Nehemiah's God-given work was no exception. He faced one problem after another. Though our own tasks today are different, problems and difficulties will surely find us. The first thirteen verses of Nehemiah 5 shine a spotlight on a dismal financial fiasco involving the Jewish workmen. The wall-rebuilding project ground to a temporary halt while their leader guided them to a godly solution.

DISCOVERING THE WAY

In the previous chapter, Nehemiah masterfully addressed the criticism of his enemies. Today's passage uncovers an even more difficult task—allaying the criticism and fear that had arisen among his own people. New sounds of discontent were erupting within the partially completed walls of Jerusalem. Money problems were opening up deep fissures between the people, threatening the completion of their God-given task.

THE HISTORICAL SITUATION

For many years the Jews of Nehemiah's time had been gradually returning from exile to live again in Jerusalem. But, though the people were free, Jerusalem's economy had not recovered since being destroyed by the Babylonians in 606 BC. All business, trade, and farming had been either ruined or disrupted by that catastrophe. Now, the struggling economy opened a fragile fault line that ran right through the center of Israel's economic structure into the people's pocketbooks. Such a fissure could easily split open if the wrong kinds of pressures were applied. And as those pressures began to build, Israel's families began to crumble. Their cooperative will was breaking apart, and people began to blame one another in a potentially disastrous upheaval.

 Read Nehemiah 5:1–5.

Finances . . . money . . . budgets . . . shortfalls . . . lines of credit. Whether balancing the family checkbook or the nation's budget, everybody in leadership has to cope with money problems and the personnel issues that inevitably arise. In fact, financial problems are one of the greatest sources of stress in a marriage, ministry, or business.

In Nehemiah's day, financial issues caused a fault line to form, causing the Jewish people to separate from each other. In the natural world of earthquakes, movement along a fault line occurs gradually through repeated "slips." The complaints of Nehemiah's people reveal three seismic slips that caused Israel's economy to quake, the people to grumble, and the wall-rebuilding project to teeter on the brink of disaster.

The first slip was famine (Nehemiah 5:3). Lack of food forced the people to mortgage their property in order to eat. The second slip was the heavy tax exacted by King Artaxerxes (5:4). The people had to borrow money just to meet the brutal tax burden. The third slip is implied: some of the wealthier Jews were charging exorbitant interest rates (5:5). The problem was compounded when a borrower couldn't repay because the lender then began repossessing the land and crops, even taking people's children as slaves in lieu of payment.

The pressure of these three slips put an unbearable strain on the people's finances as well as their emotions. Their groaning represented the rumblings of an entire society about to break apart. Nehemiah had to act quickly to avert a disaster.

Sometimes leaders respond to financial problems by burying their heads in the sand, hoping they will just go away. When was the last time you sized up your own financial responsibilities? If you had to give an on-the-spot report of your family's, ministry's, or business's financial standing, would you have the information to do so? Why, or why not?

_____

_____

What do you think is the primary root of most financial problems people face today? Lack of adequate compensation? Unfair treatment or competition? Overspending? Debt? Something else? Defend your answer with specific examples.

_____

_____

_____

_____

Do you see any of these sources of financial stress cropping up in your own realms of leadership? Which ones?

_____

_____

_____

_____

THE LEADER'S REACTION

How did Nehemiah respond when he heard about Israel's pernicious financial problems? You might be surprised.

Read Nehemiah 5:6.

The people's complaints sparked an angry response in Nehemiah that, according to the Hebrew word *charah*, "burned down inside him." He was sizzling with anger. That isn't the compassionate response we might expect from Nehemiah or any other leader! But sometimes anger is the best response. In this situation, it was both appropriate and effective. To understand why, consider Israel's legal guide and practical policy manual for running a building project: the Law of Moses, found primarily in the books of Exodus, Leviticus, and Deuteronomy.

Read Exodus 22:25 and Deuteronomy 23:19–20. Summarize the appropriate lending practices for God's people.

_____

_____

_____

_____

Read Leviticus 25:35–43. Summarize the appropriate practices regarding slavery.

_____

_____

_____

_____

How had the Israelites disregarded both the letter and the spirit of these principles?

_____

_____

_____

What were the results of their failure to abide by the principles God had given them?

_____

_____

_____

An examination of the Old Testament law reveals that though it was not wrong to lend money or charge interest to non-Jews, Jews were not to charge interest when lending money to each other. Also, it was acceptable for a Jew to render services to a lender in payment of a debt, but slavery was absolutely prohibited between Jews. And even if a Jew sold himself to another Jew as a hired worker, the Law of Moses declared that all workers must be released in the year of Jubilee.

According to the Hebrew calendar, every fiftieth year was to be celebrated as the Jubilee year, the "year of liberty" (Ezekiel 46:17). During this year,

> All property . . . which the owner had been obliged to sell
> through poverty . . . was to revert without payment to its
> original owner or his lawful heirs. . . . Every Israelite, who
> through poverty had sold himself to one of his countrymen
> or to a foreigner settled in the land . . . was to go out free
> with his children.[1]

Failure to follow these simple rules would result in economic and social consequences . . . such as the problems detailed in Nehemiah 5. Given this background, it's no wonder that Nehemiah's first response was righteous anger. If the people had followed the Law of Moses and done what was just and right in the area of finances, these problems would never have erupted.

Nehemiah wasn't angry because the people had interrupted the completion of the wall or because they had made him look bad in front of his enemies. He was angry because the people were knowingly and willfully disobeying the Law. God established those rules and regulations to set the Israelites apart as a witness of Himself.

Nehemiah didn't react by spewing out his anger indiscriminately. Nehemiah 5:7 says he first consulted with himself. He sorted out the issues and channeled the flow of his red-hot convictions directly at the problems.

THE PRACTICAL SOLUTION

In Nehemiah 5:7–13, Nehemiah chose to address the people's financial pressures by skillfully realigning their practices to conform again to the Law of Moses.

 Read Nehemiah 5:7–9.

Nehemiah leveled three accusations at the nobles and the rulers, those responsible for taking financial advantage of the people. First, he indicted them for charging outrageous interest to fellow Jews (Nehemiah 5:7). Next, he charged them with allowing permanent slavery of Jewish debtors (5:8). Finally, he accused them of losing their distinction in the eyes of the surrounding nations (5:9). Their willful disobedience brought reproach on the Lord from the pagan world around them. Nehemiah brought their illegal practices before the standard of God's Law, and the accused were convicted on all three counts. Their reaction indicates that Nehemiah presented an airtight case: "They were silent and could not find a word to say" (5:8).

 Read Nehemiah 5:10–13.

As a godly leader, Nehemiah didn't simply hurl a few rebukes and then walk away. He went on to propose some constructive changes that can apply to all situations in which wrong has been done.

1. Determine to stop the wrong (Nehemiah 5:10).
2. Make specific plans to correct the wrong immediately, regardless of the sacrifice involved (5:11).
3. Declare your plans for correction in a promise before God as the nobles and the rulers did before the priests (5:12).
4. Realize the seriousness of your promise (5:13).

In Nehemiah 5:13, the people responded with a resounding "Amen" to Nehemiah's proposals and began walking on the firm ground of God's Word.

STARTING YOUR JOURNEY

Finances cause tremors in many people's lives. Marriages, homes, businesses, and even churches collapse because of shaky money management. Consider these four solid insights as you build a financial foundation that won't buckle under pressure.

First, *God is pleased with the wise handling of our money.* God has left us ample materials in His Word for building solid financial principles into our lives. From Genesis to Revelation, money matters take up a great deal of space. In fact, some scholars have shown that the subject of money is spoken to more often than the subjects of both heaven and hell.[2]

Compare Paul's attitude toward money in Philippians 4:11–19 and 2 Corinthians 6:10 with the ruler's attitude toward money in Matthew 19:16–22. Which attitude mirrors your own? Which of your actions and financial decisions support your answer? Give specific examples.

_____

_____

_____

_____

_____

Second, *prolonged personal sin takes a heavy toll on the public work of God.* Technically, the people's finances had nothing to do with the stones and mortar of the construction project. Yet, on the practical side, their sin caused the entire project to grind to a halt.

Reflect on your current realms of leadership. What are your weaknesses or potential pitfalls when it comes to finances? Sometimes leaders can develop "blind spots" in certain areas. Consider asking a trusted Christian friend or financial counselor for his or her perspective.

_____

_____

_____

_____

How could these weaknesses affect the goals you're trying to accomplish?

_____

_____

_____

If you are a leader in a business or organization, what can you do to help those under your guidance develop sound financial habits?

_____

_____

_____

_____

How can you teach solid financial principles to your family?

_____

_____

_____

_____

Third, *correcting sin in our lives begins with facing it head-on.* Many of us spend so much time excusing and rationalizing our sin that we muffle the convicting voice of the Holy Spirit. Rather than dodging sinful attitudes about our dealings with money, we need to develop a righteous disgust for such things and actively root them out.

Are you allowing any sinful attitudes about money to go unchecked? Are you struggling with areas of unwise financial dealings in your personal life? What are they? What must you do to acknowledge and confront these issues?

_____

_____

_____

Fourth, *correction is often carried out more effectively when we make a public promise.* Like the Israelite rulers before the priests, share your commitment to change with someone who knows you well. Confide in an intimate friend or a trusted Bible-study group, people who can encourage you and help solidify your resolve to be more obedient to the Lord with your finances.

Financial accountability is not easy, but it's absolutely necessary. What systems of financial accountability do you currently have in place to protect yourself from making unwise decisions?

_____

_____

_____

Do you need greater accountability in your finances? Name some people you can trust as consultants or confidants as you seek to honor the Lord with your money.

_____

_____

_____

_____

Money problems and financial stresses can bring businesses, ministries, governments, and families to a halt. Following wise, biblical financial principles may feel like drudgery when so much more urgent work needs to be done. However, the lessons from Nehemiah's experience demonstrate the importance of godly financial accountability. If your finances lie in disarray, now is the time to set them in order.

LESSON EIGHT

How to Handle a Promotion

Nehemiah 5:14–19

THE HEART OF THE MATTER

Handling the Disappointment of Downsizing . . . Coming to Grips with Discouragement . . . Life after a Layoff. But . . . *The Pitfalls of Promotion?* We've all experienced or witnessed demotions, cutbacks, downsizes, or layoffs—dreadful realities that prompt a run on self-help books. Occasionally, however, God promotes His people in a marked fashion, but we seldom hear messages or read books about what God says to those who have experienced a promotion. So, using Nehemiah's own experience as the basis for our examination, let's learn the tests of integrity that come with a promotion.

DISCOVERING THE WAY

What is the greatest adversity that could befall you? Sickness? Financial loss? Family problems? Surprisingly, your worst adversity may be prosperity—a difficult trial hidden in designer sheep's clothing.

One writer has said, "Adversity is sometimes hard upon a man; but for one man who can stand prosperity, there are a hundred that will stand adversity."[1]

Why? Because few people being promoted up the ladder of success are able to maintain their spiritual equilibrium. The dizzying heights of prosperity often lead to pride and then a fall.

From your own experience or from someone in the media, relate an example of somebody whose promotion "went to his or her head."

_____

_____

_____

_____

_____

Specifically, why do you think it is sometimes difficult to handle a promotion with integrity?

_____

_____

_____

_____

Have you, personally, ever been promoted, only to uncover unknown weaknesses in yourself? Describe this experience and how it affected you.

_____

_____

_____

PROMOTION: AN AXIOM TO REMEMBER

In just a few well-crafted lines, Psalm 75:5–7 strikes both a chord and a nerve for all who long for promotions, fret when they're passed over, or weep when they're demoted:

> " 'Do not lift up your horn on high,
> Do not speak with insolent pride.' "

> For not from the east, nor from the west,
> Nor from the desert comes exaltation;
> But God is the Judge;
> *He puts down one, and exalts another.*
> (Psalm 75:5–7, emphasis added)

GETTING TO THE ROOT
The Author of Promotion

In the Hebrew text of Psalm 75:5–7 we find three words all derived from the same root: *rum.* The first, *lamarōm,* translated "on high"[2] (75:5), refers to a sense of arrogance, self-exaltation. The word *hariym,* or "exaltation" (75:6), describes the process of ascending from a lower to higher place.[3] Exaltation does not come from anything in this world, though worldly minded people may believe it does. Where does *hariym* truly come from? Verse 6 says that God is the One who "exalts" (*yariym*). But Psalm 75 makes an important contrast and clarification. God is also the One who "puts down." So both promotion and demotion come from God—not from the world or from our own doing.

In describing the much-coveted process of promotion, the psalmist forged a timeless truth: the promotion of every child of God comes by God's sovereign grace, not because a person is in the right place at the right time, morally good, more gifted, well-educated, or highly trained.

The Bible is full of good examples. Some leaders, such as Joseph, kept their heads after being promoted. God promoted Joseph from prisoner in Egypt to preeminent ruler over Pharaoh's empire. And God exalted Daniel, a Hebrew exile taken to Babylon, where he was appointed to be King Nebuchadnezzar's right-hand man. God even promoted Amos, a rugged country farmer with fig-stained hands, to go before the polished priest Amaziah and announce God's judgment. These three men maintained their integrity in spite of their promotions. And they refused to demote God from His position as Lord of their lives.

But perhaps the best illustration of someone responsibly handling a promotion is Nehemiah. Even though he was born and reared in a time when the Jewish people were living in captivity to another nation, God exalted him to the prominent place of cupbearer to King Artaxerxes (Nehemiah 1:11). And when Nehemiah voluntarily took a demotion to rebuild Jerusalem's wall, God had another promotion in store.

God promotes and demotes according to His perfect will. Read the following passages, then note what each one declares about God's character as it relates to His choice to raise up or bring low.

1 Samuel 2:7–8

_____

_____

Job 12:16–25

_____

_____

Psalm 147:5–6

_____

_____

Daniel 2:20–22

_____

_____

Based on these passages, why are people promoted or demoted?

_____

_____

PROMOTION: AN EXAMPLE TO FOLLOW

In the midst of gates being rebuilt, stones replaced, and enemies rebuffed, it became apparent to the people that Nehemiah was an outstanding leader. So they promoted him to the highest office in the land of Judah—governor.

 Read Nehemiah 5:14–16.

Nehemiah accepted his promotion, even though he surely knew he was stepping out of the frying pan and into the fire. What makes this moment in Scripture significant? He said "yes" to God.

Strange as it may sound, many of the most gifted, qualified Christians today seem reluctant to step into leadership positions. Why? Sometimes they view it as an inconvenience. Other times fear or feelings of inadequacy get the better of them. Some believe it's more spiritual to hide in the shadows or work behind the scenes. Or they may view a promotion to a prominent responsibility as a sign of selfish ambition or carnality. But when wise, godly men and women say "no" to becoming college professors, university presidents, business executives, filmmakers, governors, senators, or other leaders who mold and shape the minds of the people, the Christian community loses the opportunity to have godly influence in strategic positions. We desperately need uncompromising Christians in all levels of leadership and in all realms of society (Proverbs 29:2).

Nehemiah was a wise, godly leader who said "yes" when God cast His decisive vote in his favor. As soon as he had accepted the appointment as governor, though, he was hit with the same four major areas of testing that come with every promotion: *privileges, policies, projects,* and *people.* And the key to surviving this onslaught is integrity. Integrity is "a firm adherence to a code of . . . values; . . . the quality or state of being complete or undivided."[4]

Privileges. Every promotion comes equipped with its own special set of privileges, rights, benefits, and special favors. Few can resist using them without abusing them. Nehemiah did not abuse his privileges; he chose instead to exhibit integrity.

"For twelve years, neither I nor my kinsmen have eaten the governor's food allowance" (Nehemiah 5:14). Although Nehemiah had the right to indulge and enjoy a sumptuous diet built into the governor's budget, he restrained himself—over a long period of time. With the people still facing hardship, Nehemiah exercised self-control and refused to presume on his office and the people.

In contrast, in 2 Samuel 15:1–6 we find an example of someone who couldn't handle a promotion. When David appointed his son Absalom to a leadership position, Absalom used it to steal the hearts of the people so he could overthrow his own father. Rather than use his position to help shepherd the people, Absalom used his privileges to feed the greedy desires of his own heart.

When we contrast this sacrifice of privilege with the self-indulgent lifestyle of David's power-hungry son, Absalom, Nehemiah's character shines. Nehemiah refused to take advantage of his position. Absalom exploited his.

Consider your personal realms of leadership. Are you presuming upon privileges in any specific areas? What are they?

_____

_____

_____

Read 1 Corinthians 9:11–15 and 10:23–33. Paul sacrificed his personal privileges as an apostle for the good of those under his leadership. How might your own sacrifice of rightful benefits or privileges have an impact on your area of leadership?

_____

_____

_____

Policies. Nearly every promotion carries with it the pressure of former policies, as shown by the first eight words of Nehemiah 5:15: "But the former governors who were before me." No matter what the position, almost all promotions involve stepping into someone else's shoes and policies. And that means pressure to do what has always been done or pressure to try something new. In his new job, Nehemiah faced three corrupt policies passed on from his predecessors. They had enforced heavy taxes, extorted food and money, and allowed their servants to oppress the people. The political and social scavengers who fed off this way of life surely put pressure on Nehemiah to look the other way. But we can see Nehemiah's resolve in just one sentence: "I did not do so because of the fear of God" (5:15).

If you're in a leadership position that someone else previously occupied, list three similarities and three differences between your policies and practices and theirs.

Similarities

_____

_____

_____

Differences

_____

_____

_____

How have the policies that changed or the practices that remained the same been helpful to those who serve under your guidance? Or how have they been harmful?

_____

_____

_____

_____

Projects. Not only did Nehemiah avoid taking advantage of the people, he also didn't slack off on his God-given work (Nehemiah 5:16). He and his servants weren't there to buy land for themselves or accumulate power or wealth; they were there with a goal in mind. Although his newfound political position afforded great opportunity for distraction, Nehemiah never lost sight of his primary task—rebuilding the walls of Jerusalem.

 Read Nehemiah 5:17–18.

People. With more than one hundred and fifty people to feed at his table every day, including officials from surrounding nations (5:17–18), Nehemiah could easily have become concerned with parties, politics, and protocol, forgetting about his God-given work. Or he could have become so obsessed with the project that he forgot about the needs of the people. Nehemiah exhibited an important balance.

Every leadership position involves dealing with people—serving them, handling their needs, and entering into their hurts. Nevertheless, many leaders don't think twice about running over other people in order to accomplish their own objectives. Projects are important, but without people, tasks crumble. Nehemiah resisted the temptation to mistreat or neglect his people or to regard his needs as more important than theirs. Even in the glory of governorship, Nehemiah "did not demand the governor's food allowance, *because the servitude was heavy on this people*" (5:18, emphasis added).

Seeing that the people were already overburdened and overtaxed because of the pace and magnitude of the project, he adjusted his leadership to lighten their load, helping to ensure completion of the task. J. Oswald Sanders, in his book, *Spiritual Leadership*, says:

> The man who is impatient with weakness will be defective in his leadership. The evidence of our strength lies not in racing ahead, but in a willingness to adapt our stride to the slower

pace of our weaker brethren while not forfeiting our lead. If we run too far ahead, we lose our power to influence.[5]

Do you struggle with the relationship between people and projects? Do you tend to prioritize one over the other? Which one, and why?

_____

_____

_____

If people and projects are in proper balance, what does that relationship look like?

_____

_____

_____

 Read Nehemiah 5:19.

All too often, when a person is promoted to a place of prominence, his or her relationship with the Lord suffers, sometimes quite severely. It would have been easy for Nehemiah to neglect his relationship with the Lord, as so many kings and rulers before him had. Yet because of his reverence for God, he restrained himself (5:15). Nehemiah maintained his integrity before God and before others. And as the pressures increased, he rested His heart and mind on the Lord (5:19).

STARTING YOUR JOURNEY

Every promotion tests the integrity of leaders in the areas of privileges, policies, projects, and people. Chances are, this lesson has surfaced some issues regarding your own struggles with one or more of these tests. Quickly review your answers to the questions in this lesson. Then complete the following chart, assigning yourself a letter grade for each area and explaining why you assigned yourself that grade.

Test	Grade	Explanation
Privileges		
Policies		
Projects		
People		

Read Job 31:5–8 and Psalm 139:23–24. For the sake of your integrity before God and others, what changes can you make to improve your response to the tests of promotion? Set out several specific actions below and design a plan to implement them.

_____

_____

_____

_____

_____

If you are a leader waiting to be promoted, could it be that God has you in a holding pattern for a reason? How might you prepare yourself now to face the tests of potential promotion?

_____

_____

_____

_____

_____

If you have recently been demoted, what is your response to learning about how Nehemiah faced the tests of promotion? What has the Lord been teaching you through this?

_____

_____

_____

Demotions can surely bring despair . . . but promotions can bring devastation to a person's integrity before God and others. When God raises up believers to positions of authority, their integrity will be tested in the areas of privileges, policies, projects, and people. When we're faced with a promotion, we should step into Nehemiah's sandals and become that one in a hundred who can handle a promotion well.

LESSON NINE

Operation Intimidation

Nehemiah 6

THE HEART OF THE MATTER

For months Nehemiah led the project of rebuilding Jerusalem's walls in spite of constant opposition, both subtle and overt. As the walls neared completion (Nehemiah 6:1), threatening foes once again assailed this leader. But this time the attack was much more insidious than before; the enemy attempted to intimidate Nehemiah through several frightening plots. But because Nehemiah had developed God-given discernment, none of these plans succeeded . . . and the wall was completed.

DISCOVERING THE WAY

A well-known cartoon series chronicles the endless frustration of a hapless coyote who can't quite catch up with the object of his culinary obsession. Try as he might, no "perfect" scheme, no elaborate trap, no ideal setup will bring him face to face with the elusive roadrunner.

Perhaps no one has tried harder and failed more miserably at destroying his target than the coyote of classic Saturday-morning cartoons. But the murderous designs of Sanballat, Tobiah, and Geshem run a close second. In real life, those wily enemies of Israel tried to trap or discredit Nehemiah again and again, with ever more creative tactics, but they endured the humiliation of one failed attempt after another. Let's zoom in to observe the troublesome trio's latest attacks . . .

The ancient equivalent of a modern ribbon-cutting ceremony was in sight, and as a feeling of euphoria washed over the people, their enemies began to focus their deceitful attacks on Nehemiah. They waited for a time when their operation of intimidation would be least expected. Though Jerusalem's main defense was almost ready, Nehemiah's personal defenses were about to be tested.

Leaders are often more susceptible to attack when intoxicated with success. Our enemies tailor personal attacks for those times when our accomplishments have us walking on air. The apostle Paul warned, "Let him who thinks he stands take heed lest he fall" (1 Corinthians 10:12).

Because of Nehemiah's rock-solid integrity, he had successfully kept the ravening enemies of Israel at bay when they tried using angry threats to interfere with the completion of the wall (Nehemiah 4:1–3). In Nehemiah 6, however, Sanballat, Tobiah, and Geshem gave up their pursuit of Israel and singled out Nehemiah himself. In four separate attacks, Nehemiah's enemies set their best traps to stop him from advancing Israel's recovery. And in all four cases, Nehemiah's wise, God-given discernment delivered him, and his perseverance sustained him.

In your own words, define *discernment.*

_____

_____

_____

_____

On a scale of 1 to 10, with 10 being the highest, how would you rate your own level of discernment according to your definition?

1   2   3   4   5   6   7   8   9   10

On what personal experiences do you base both your definition and your grade?

_____

_____

_____

Defined as "a power to see what is not evident to the average mind, discernment stresses accuracy (as in reading character or motives)."[1] In Proverbs 8, discernment goes hand in hand with wisdom and prudence ("skill and good judgment in the use of resources"[2])—all godly qualities that are essential to leadership.

WHAT WERE THE FOUR ATTACKS?

In Nehemiah 6, Nehemiah carefully described the four different kinds of attacks his enemies used to try to intimidate him: a personal request, a public letter, a subtle conspiracy, and threatening communication.

 Read Nehemiah 6:1–4.

The first attack launched on Nehemiah came in the guise of a harmless *personal request* (Nehemiah 6:2). Despite all their antagonistic efforts,

Nehemiah's enemies had been unable to defeat him. So Sanballat and Geshem crafted a syrupy invitation, hoping to lure Nehemiah using a gracious ploy. Their language suggested that the visit would be as warm as a family reunion. And the verdant valley of Ono, only twenty miles away, would have been a welcome relief from the rugged stonework in Jerusalem.

But somewhere behind those placating words, Nehemiah smelled the scent of the wily coyote (Nehemiah 6:2). How was Nehemiah able to do this? He possessed the crucial leadership skill of discernment. Without it, the book of Nehemiah might have ended with a funeral in the valley of Ono.

Not only did Nehemiah discern his enemies' treachery, he also sensed another danger: the potential for a delay or stoppage in the work (Nehemiah 6:3). One of the signs of a mature leader is the ability to say no. Nehemiah sensed the cold heart behind the warm invitation, and he kept himself free from the trap with a firm no. He said it not just once, but four times (6:4).

A servant of God is never required to be a puppet of man. In other words, a commitment to ministry does not automatically imply an obligation to please people. A wise, discerning leader must be strong enough to say no to some, perhaps most, requests for his or her time and attention . . . even without an explanation. For most over-achievers or people-pleasers, saying no once is hard enough, but to follow Nehemiah's example and say it four times can be excruciating. Whenever possible, leaders should establish a policy of taking time to weigh decisions before saying yes.

Why do you think people in leadership often have a hard time saying no? List a few positive and negative motivators that drive many leaders to say yes more frequently than they should.

Positive	Negative
_____	_____
_____	_____
_____	_____
_____	_____

What are some negative consequences of saying yes too often?

_____

_____

_____

_____

In your own experience, how does discernment play a role in determining when to say yes and when to say no?

_____

_____

_____

_____

 Read Nehemiah 6:5–9.

After four unsuccessful attempts, Sanballat decided to shift from a diplomatic invitation to political propaganda in the form of an open letter for everyone to read as it snaked its way to its recipient. Nehemiah may have even known the contents of the letter before it arrived, thanks to the speedy courier service of the gossip grapevine. The widely publicized letter basically alleged that Nehemiah intended to lead a revolt and set himself up as king. At first glance, it appeared that Nehemiah could not escape being impaled on the horns of Sanballat's baseless rumors. If he refused to go to Ono, it would be tantamount to admitting his guilt. But if he went to Ono, he'd be walking into a trap.

DIGGING DEEPER

Masterful Manipulation

Let's step back for a moment and examine the underlying characteristics of Sanballat's letter—the same traits we find in all tales churned out by the rumor mill. First, *the source of a rumor is often unknown.* Nehemiah 6:6 says, "It is reported." Who reported it? If it's a rumor, usually no one quite knows. Second, *rumors are filled with exaggeration and inaccuracy.* Sanballat declared that this news was being discussed among "the nations," but it was likely limited to the grapevine in and around Jerusalem. Third, *rumors lead to personal hurt and misunderstanding.* Even though it isn't implicitly stated in these verses, whenever a person's integrity is impugned, it hurts. Rumors are designed to cause pain. Finally, *rumors are employed by those whose motives are evil.* "So come now, let us take counsel together" (6:7). Sanballat was still eager to arrange for Nehemiah's one-way trip to Ono.

Gossip and its close cousins, slander and libel, are all part of a large family of insidious sins that include other prominent members such as greed, envy, murder, strife, and deceit (Romans 1:29; 2 Corinthians 12:20; 2 Timothy 3:3). One author sums up the problem with gossip well:

People are always quick to believe the worst about others. Think, if you will, of how quickly scandal spreads through an office or a church. The faintest hint at indiscreet behavior and the person concerned is pronounced guilty. . . . The libel may be totally false, yet it is impossible for the victim of such [vicious gossip] ever to clear his name with everyone who gives ear to the reports.[3]

Regardless of how well a leader may manage people and projects, the unseen sin of gossip can eat away at any person's credibility. And just as we wouldn't put up with murder in the workplace, so as leaders, we must shield ourselves and our people against the character assassination that comes with gossip.

If you're wondering how to respond when the rumor is about you, Nehemiah's methods for handling gossip, beginning in verse 8, provide a good example.

First, *he calmly denied the charge* (Nehemiah 6:8).
Second, *he put the blame where it belonged* (6:8).
Third, *he took his hurt to God* (6:9).

When you run into someone spilling out rumors, a loving rebuke is the best response. Plug up the informational leak with a gentle yet firm reproof. And seek comfort from the One who knows and sees the truth.

As you review the three steps Nehemiah took in dealing with gossip, how do you see discernment functioning in these actions?

_____

_____

_____

What might a foolish and impulsive response have looked like? What would have been the result?

_____

_____

_____

_____

 Read Nehemiah 6:10–14.

The next attack from the enemy was perhaps the most ingenious. Having failed at their two previous attempts, Nehemiah's enemies donned a saintly guise and baptized their evil intentions in pious words! They sought to catch Nehemiah with his guard down in the place he was most likely to feel secure, the temple. But again, Nehemiah's discernment enabled him to see the enemy's snare camouflaged beneath the false piety. He recognized the attack as the deceitful trap it was, and then he wisely turned his anger over to the Lord.

 Read Nehemiah 6:15–19.

The wall was finally finished! The schemes of Sanballat and Geshem had been thwarted . . . but before any celebrations could begin, more opposition arose. Tobiah was busy conducting guerrilla warfare of his own with a barrage of letters designed to intimidate Nehemiah.

People in leadership receive all kinds of correspondence, and much of it is critical in nature. Nasty notes, rude e-mails, captious text messages, belligerent voicemails, or even old-fashioned hate mail—they can demoralize or intimidate leaders who may already be reeling under a barrage of personal attacks. If you have experienced something similar, you know that one mean-spirited comment can trump a dozen glowing praises. Leaders need discernment to help them weed out the wicked comments designed to discourage and to focus instead on the legitimate concerns that need real attention. And there's just one place for unsigned letters or anonymous notes: the trash bin.

WHAT WERE THE EFFECTS OF THE ATTACKS?

The campaign of intimidation by Nehemiah's enemies certainly put Nehemiah's discernment to the test, impacting both his personal life and the work God gave him to do. Because Nehemiah stayed on his knees, he was able to face the threats without giving in to them or losing sight of his ultimate goal. And Nehemiah matched his enemies' commitment to harassment with his own relentless commitment to finishing the wall (Nehemiah 6:15–16).

In short, Nehemiah exposed "Operation Intimidation" using his discernment, and he battled against it with determination.

 STARTING YOUR JOURNEY
Over and over again Nehemiah avoided the traps set by his enemies by exercising discernment. Without that, Nehemiah and Israel's promising future might well have been buried in the valley of Ono. Perhaps your desire to lead effectively and efficiently has been jeopardized by a lack of discernment. Maybe you've trusted people you should have doubted or kept your distance when you should have invested. Perhaps you hired a scoundrel or overlooked the gifts and abilities of a quality employee. Developing and applying discernment in leadership is essential. Let's take a few moments to study Nehemiah's source of discernment, which can also be our own.

According to the following verses, where does discernment come from?

1 Kings 4:29–30   Psalm 119:65–66   Philippians 1:9–10

_____   _____   _____

_____   _____   _____

Besides the knowledge of God's Word, what is necessary for developing discernment? (See Hebrews 5:14.)

_____

What must you do to develop this kind of discernment in your life?

_____

_____

_____

_____

If your discernment skills are still developing, you need to gather trusted support to complement you in this area. As you think about those closest to you—perhaps in your family, ministry, or work environments—can you identify a few people who seem to have an extra measure of discernment? How do they exhibit discernment in their lives?

_____

_____

_____

What can you do to benefit from their skills in the area of discernment?

_____

_____

_____

_____

Nehemiah overcame tests of deception, gossip, and intimidation through his God-given, experience-sharpened discernment. With tenacious determination, he was able to navigate his project to completion. We, too, need discernment to persevere through the inevitable challenges in our own realms of leadership.

LESSON TEN

Revival at Water Gate?

Nehemiah 8:1–12

THE HEART OF THE MATTER

Once the walls and gates were finally completed (Nehemiah 6:15), Nehemiah organized Jerusalem into a well-guarded, stable body of people (7:1–73). Immediately upon the completion of this massive task, he made plans to revive the authority of the Scriptures in the minds of the citizens. The testimony of God's Word had been silent for far too long. The beginnings of spiritual revival were taking place. And the potential for revival is always present in our own lives, if we just know where to look.

DISCOVERING THE WAY

Mention the word *revival* today and many people immediately think of crowds of people packed into tents, tin-roofed chapels, or stadiums, while wildly gesturing evangelists preach fire and brimstone. Some may picture a white-suited preacher flanked by an enthusiastic choir, pacing back and forth on stage, waving his Bible like a spiritual weapon, and shouting "hallelu-hee-YAH" before and after every sentence as he proclaims the gospel with fervor to lost souls.

But actually, revivals do not pertain to unbelievers, but to *believers*—those who have already been made alive through faith in Christ. It is impossible to "revive" the lost—they need to be saved. (If you're not certain about whether you need to be revived or saved, please read "How to Begin a Relationship with God" at the end of this book.) Like smelling salts, a revival can restore believers whose love for the Lord has grown faint. After weakened Christians have been revived through the proclamation of God's Word, they exhibit a new passion for the things of God and often begin to share the gospel with others. Some Christians schedule annual revivals, others pray for revivals, and still others are surprised when revivals happen.

As you ponder your enthusiasm for God's Word, do you think your current attitudes and actions are greater, lesser, or the same as when you first became a believer?

greater   the same   lesser

If they have changed, why do you think this is the case?

_____

_____

_____

If a person were to grade your dependence on God's Word for the discernment, growth, and encouragement necessary for successful leadership, how do you think they would rate you based on outward observation?

1   2   3   4   5   6   7   8   9   10

How would you rate yourself?

| 1 | 2 | 3 | 4 | 5 | 6 | 7 | 8 | 9 | 10 |

THE SETTING FOR REVIVAL

Having completed the wall and elected Nehemiah as governor, the people of Israel were well-organized, well-defended, and well-governed (Nehemiah 7). But their spiritual welfare still languished from neglect. So they asked Ezra to meet with them in what would prove to be the beginning of a legendary spiritual revival.

 Read Nehemiah 8:1–2.

The people met at the square in front of the Water Gate. One of the key figures at this gathering was Ezra, a godly scribe and priest. As a scribe, Ezra possessed expertise in two areas. He was an expert in the realm of legal matters, able to act as both judge and jury before the people, and he was an expert in interpreting Scripture—able to teach the Word of God. As a priest, Ezra was responsible for going into the temple to represent the people before God.

According to verse 2, the people *voluntarily* came together, seeking spiritual food from the Law of Moses after decades of hunger for its nourishing power. This revival took place "on the first day of the seventh month" (Nehemiah 8:2). What's so significant about the timing? For the Jews, that day marked the beginning of their most sacred month of the year, in which they celebrated three important feasts: the Feast of Trumpets, the Feast of Atonement, and the Feast of Booths. Traditionally, the Scriptures were read on the first day of the Feast of Booths, so after hundreds of years, the Israelites started fresh—with obedience.

Read the following verses and fill in the chart below.

Passage	Benefits of Reading the Word of God
Deuteronomy 11:18–21	
Psalm 19:7–11	
2 Timothy 3:15–17	
Hebrews 4:12	

Based on your observations above, how should reading God's Word affect your leadership?

_____

_____

_____

THE EVENT OF REVIVAL

After United States Air Force pilot Howard Rutledge was shot down over North Vietnam, he spent the rest of the war fighting to survive as a prisoner of war in a foreign land. Like the Israelites, Rutledge became acutely aware of his spiritual hunger pains:

> Now the sights and sounds and smells of death were all around me. My hunger for spiritual food soon outdid my hunger for a steak. Now I wanted to know about that part

of me that will never die. Now I wanted to talk about God
and Christ and the church. But in Heartbreak [prison
camp] solitary confinement, there was no pastor, no
Sunday-school teacher, no Bible, no hymnbook, no community of believers to guide and sustain me.[1]

Perhaps Rutledge's experience can give us a glimpse into the emotion of
that moment when Israel, after seventy years of captivity and being cut off
from knowing the Lord as their forefathers had known Him, gathered
together to hear Ezra explain God's Law.

 Read Nehemiah 8:3–8.

Nehemiah 8:3–8 contains a detailed account of the exposition of
Scripture that the people heard that day. That exposition had three distinct
characteristics.

First, *the exposition included reading of the Scriptures.* Ezra read to the
nation of former prisoners of war the life-giving Word they had so sorely
missed. He read to them for several hours as the people stood and listened in
silent awe (Nehemiah 8:3–5).

Second, *the exposition included praise because of the Scriptures.* Ezra praised
God for what He had revealed to them in His Word (Nehemiah 8:6). The
Israelites then responded in a spontaneous, unguarded expression of praise
and gratitude. Only those whose deepest spiritual needs have been satisfied
know how to give that kind of praise.

Third, *the exposition included insight into the Scriptures.* These verses strike
a beautiful balance between the emotional and the intellectual. Had the people
gorged themselves on only the good feelings that accompanied that day, they
would have immediately felt hungry again. Instead, each Israelite received a

large, satiating helping of the Word through the teaching ministry of Ezra and the Levites (Nehemiah 8:7–8).

Even though the Israelites listening that day were Jews by birth and heritage, their people had lived under captivity in Babylon for at least seventy years. Their mind-set had been shaped by the Chaldean culture around them. They had learned to speak Aramaic rather than the Hebrew of their fathers. So after Ezra read the Law in Hebrew, the Levites translated it, teaching and explaining the meaning of the words and passages so the people could understand and apply the Law to their lives. That day at the Water Gate was like a massive relief effort. Ezra came fully supplied with God's Word, and the Levites fed the people. And the difference was immediately visible. Israel's spiritual vital signs began to revive.

Do you sometimes feel so spiritually distant from God that it feels as though you need an interpreter? Just as it takes time and exposure to learn a new language, so it takes time and exposure to understand God's Word. His Word is the primary way He speaks to us. For each day of the last week, estimate how much time you spent in Bible study, prayer, and worship.

	Bible Study	Prayer	Worship
Sunday			
Monday			
Tuesday			
Wednesday			
Thursday			
Friday			
Saturday			

According to your own experience, what are the benefits of setting a consistent place and time for reading and studying the Bible?

_____

_____

_____

According to James 1:22, 25 and Hebrews 2:1, summarize in your own words the perils of not reading or heeding God's Word.

_____

_____

_____

Do you have a specific place and time set aside to spend with the Lord, reading His Word? If so, what is it? If not, have you ever tried to set one? What seems to get in the way?

_____

_____

_____

What is the greatest obstacle that prevents you from spending more time in these areas?

_____

_____

_____

THE MOBILIZATION OF GOD'S PEOPLE

One of the first visible signs of revival that day in Israel were the tears of guilt and regret shed by the people as they faced the severity of their sins.

Read Nehemiah 8:9–12.

The remnant of Israel wept over the sins of their forefathers that had led them into captivity. Then, when the Law of Moses was explained to them for the first time in decades, the people not only became reacquainted with their own laws and sacrifices, but they were also reintroduced to Yahweh, the holy God of Israel. In the light of His perfect presence, their own great sins broke their hearts.

Certainly, this kind of guilt is wholly appropriate. But the people needed to move on from feeling remorse to knowing the joy of God's grace and forgiveness. So Ezra, Nehemiah, and the Levites, as loving ministers of God's Word, moved their people from mourning to celebration . . . from grief to joy (Nehemiah 8:10–12).

Though the day had begun with spiritual hunger, it ended with satisfaction, forgiveness, and rejoicing. The people of God had been revived.

 STARTING YOUR JOURNEY

Before we leave this incredible scene of revival at Water Gate, let's pause to consider four practical lessons.

First, *no life is complete without spiritual dimension.* Many of us are like the Israelites—we have well-organized lives and homes, but we lack a vibrant spiritual life. We feel the pangs of emptiness as Howard Rutledge did in the Vietnamese prison camp. We feel the same aches as the spiritually starving people of Israel. And if we don't fill that hunger with God's Word, we'll naturally try to fill it with something else. Augustine once confessed to God, "You have made us for yourself, and our heart is restless until it rests in you."[2]

Second, *no spiritual dimension is complete without scriptural input.* Just as our physical bodies depend on food to sustain them, our spiritual lives depend on the food supplied by God's Word. The Lord Jesus, quoting Deuteronomy 8:3, confirmed this truth: "Man shall not live on bread alone, but on every word that proceeds out of the mouth of God" (Matthew 4:4).

Third, *no scriptural input is complete without personal obedience.* Hearing the truths of Scripture without acting upon them is like sitting down to a feast without partaking. The people of Israel not only heard the Word of God, they acted upon it. First they restored the reading of the Word, and then, as we will discover in the next lesson, they reinstituted a God-ordained feast. They personally digested what they heard, allowing God to nourish their hearts.

Fourth, *no personal obedience is complete without great rejoicing.* Rejuvenated by the first solid spiritual food they had ingested in years, the people of Israel dried their tears, gathered their children, and headed home with a feeling of euphoria that rivaled the day they completed the construction of the walls. They were exuberant in their restored relationship with God.

The discernment, character, and encouragement necessary to lead with wisdom and integrity come from regularly feeding on the Word of God. Select one or two suggestions from the following list, then in the space below, describe how you will start this week.[3]

_____ **Hear the Word of God.** Listen to an audio version of the Bible in the car, at the gym, or at home after a busy day.

_____ **Read the Word of God.** Select a daily Bible-reading program; try reading from different Bible versions; or establish a nightly Bible-reading time with your family after dinner.

_____ **Study the Word of God.** Use a trustworthy study Bible or guide to make observations from the text, discuss the Bible in a small group, or read books or commentaries to help you better understand specific passages.

_____ **Memorize the Word of God.** Psalm 119:11 emphasizes the memorization of Scripture. As you hear, read, and study God's Word, some memorization will come naturally. Select key passages you want to commit to memory, then write them down and bring them with you everywhere until you learn them.

_____ **Meditate on the Word of God.** Joshua 1:8 and Psalm 119:148 refer to pondering how Scripture relates to your life, reminding yourself of it daily, discussing it with others, and allowing your heart to absorb it as you run it through your mind throughout the day.

Your commitment:
"I plan to implement my choice this week by . . .

_____

_____

_____

_____

If your greatest struggle is merely having the desire to read God's Word, ask God to develop a passion in your heart for it. Write your prayer for spiritual revival below.

_____

_____

_____

_____

Revival of our spiritual lives comes when we understand and apply God's Word in our lives. When we hear, read, study, memorize, and meditate on His Word, we partake of spiritual food that will ultimately grow us into the godly servant leaders He wants us to be. Just as Nehemiah's people flourished once they were exposed to the reviving power of God's Word, your own revival awaits.

LESSON ELEVEN

The Fine Art of Insight

Nehemiah 8:13–18

THE HEART OF THE MATTER

The spiritual revival led by Ezra at the Water Gate (Nehemiah 8:1–12) was just the beginning of the Israelites' desire to remodel themselves before the Lord. In search of a solid foundation in the Law, they returned to Ezra, seeking insight—wisdom that could be built into their daily lives. They committed to clear away the rubble of wrong thinking and their old patterns of living, replacing them with obedience to the Lord and His Law. This biblical method for spiritual renovation is an excellent model for rebuilding our spiritual lives today.

DISCOVERING THE WAY

A wise man once said, "Knowledge comes, but wisdom lingers."[1] Knowledge is simply a collection of facts—what is and what was. Insight connotes a deeper understanding of what the facts imply—consequences, implications, and significance. Knowledge doesn't necessarily move easily into practice, but insight always leads directly to a response or action. It is a singular blend of knowledge and wisdom, married to decisive results.

We can all think of people with great knowledge who lack wisdom and insight. Can you think of an example of a person who possesses both knowledge and insight? How do you think that person added insight to his or her knowledge?

_____

_____

_____

Do you think it's possible for a person to have insight without knowledge? Why, or why not?

_____

_____

_____

In Hebrew the word for insight, *sakal,* means to "be prudent, circumspect."[2] One dictionary defines insight as "the power or act of seeing into a situation . . . apprehending the inner nature of things."[3] On the first day of their revival, the Israelites were given knowledge (Nehemiah 8:8). The next day, they came back "that they might gain insight" (8:13). They desired to penetrate below the surface of God's Word in search of wisdom.

THE PURSUIT OF INSIGHT

The book of Nehemiah could easily be divided into two distinct construction phases—the reconstruction of the wall (Nehemiah 1–6) and the reinstruction of the people (7–13). Both desperately needed rebuilding. In our last lesson, we observed the people's spiritual renovation in a revival led by Ezra at the Water Gate (8:1–12). But this was just the beginning of the Israelites' desire to move back into a right relationship with the Lord.

Let's take a moment to examine the five specific things necessary for the mining of that precious spiritual gem—insight.

 Read Nehemiah 8:13.

First, *gaining insight takes time.* Merely memorizing biblical facts does not automatically lead to gaining insight. It results in knowledge, but not wisdom. True insight is always hard-won; it doesn't come instantly. In Psalm 119:15, the psalmist wrote, "I will *study* your commandments and *reflect on* your ways" (NLT, emphasis added). Just as an unwise person cannot become wise overnight, it is impossible to gain insight apart from a regular intake of Scripture.

Read the following Scripture passages. What metaphors are used to describe the process of acquiring wisdom? What do they indicate about the relationship between wisdom and time?

Proverbs 2:2–6

_____

_____

Proverbs 24:3–4

_____

_____

Second, *gaining insight takes people.* Successfully pursuing insight involves learning from the right kind of person. According to Nehemiah 8:13, Ezra was the rare and essential person Israel needed. The leaders of Israel huddled at his feet to gather pearls of wisdom. His qualification as an instructor involved three ongoing tasks: "For Ezra had set his heart to *study* the law of the LORD and to *practice* it, and to *teach* His statutes and ordinances in Israel" (Ezra 7:10, emphasis added).

For years Ezra had cultivated insight by planting the seeds of God's Word in his mind through study, by watering through practicing what he learned, and by sharing the fruits through teaching others. And because of his faithfulness in these tasks, he was given the immense privilege of reinstructing God's people in His Law.

Do you have an "Ezra" in your life whom you trust to provide you with insight into understanding and applying God's Word? If so, describe how he or she exhibits Ezra's qualities. If not, seek out someone who knows the Word and lives a life marked by insight and integrity.

_____

_____

_____

_____

_____

Third, *gaining insight takes the right attitude.* According to Proverbs 13:10, "Wisdom is with those who receive counsel." The men who came to hear Ezra that day were heads of households, dads, grandfathers, priests, and Levites—all leaders in their own realm (see Nehemiah 8:13). Many were probably Ezra's age or older. Yet they did not allow their age or expertise to hinder their teachable spirits. They came with open, appreciative, even eager attitudes.

Consider your realms of leadership. Are you open to receiving godly counsel from others? Do your attitudes and actions exhibit a teachable attitude? Why, or why not?

_____

_____

_____

Have you ever ignored godly counsel because of your own pride? What happened?

_____

_____

_____

Read Nehemiah 8:14–15.

Fourth, *gaining insight takes the right source.* Ezra never intended to be the people's ultimate source of insight. After so many years of pursuing insight himself, he knew where to lead the people to find it—"they found [it] written in the law" (Nehemiah 8:14). For seventy years Israel had been forced to prospect for wisdom down the empty mine shafts of the world. Now, finally, they were ready to restake their claim as God's people and earnestly excavate from the mother lode of insight—God's Word.

In your current realms of leadership or influence—whether in the family, the church, or a business—to what or to whom do you first turn for insight when a problem arises?

_____

_____

How long do you search before turning to God's Word? Does anything keep you from seeking wisdom there first? What is it?

_____

_____

_____

Fifth, *gaining insight takes the right response.* The expectant men of Israel who gathered to search the Scriptures that day were not disappointed. They rediscovered a priceless celebration that many had forgotten—the Feast of Tabernacles (or Booths). Once they became aware of the command regarding this celebration, they immediately issued a public proclamation, conveying instructions on how to build booths in order to reinstitute the feast (Nehemiah 8:15). Clearly, the people had not been simply gaining information but were committed to adapting their lives to it. They responded with unquestioning obedience (8:14–17).

DOORWAY TO HISTORY
The Feast of Tabernacles

Memorials, monuments, and celebrations are designed to commemorate an event of deep significance. Through feasts and other holidays dictated by the Lord in the Old Testament, the people of Israel recognized the reality of God's provision and renewed their commitment to obey Him alone.

God had ordained several annual feasts in the Old Testament, each one illustrating a significant aspect of His relationship with His people. They were "memorials of God's saving acts in the past, sacraments of His sanctifying power in the present, and types of His anticipated victory over sin in the forthcoming first and second advents of Jesus Christ."[4]

The Feast of Tabernacles (or Booths) was an annual remembrance of a time when the Jews lived in temporary quarters. From the time they were delivered from slavery in Egypt under Moses until they entered Canaan under Joshua, they lived in tents. This feast was designed to remind them of the Lord's care and protection during their time in the wilderness and His promises to protect them and provide for their needs in the future. As such, they were instructed to gather branches and build small booths to live in for the seven days of the feast (Leviticus 23:33–43).

THE PRODUCTS OF INSIGHT

Israel's insight into the Law brought about three visible results. And these responses will be evident in our lives as well, when we truly seek insight from God's Word.

 Read Nehemiah 8:16–18.

The first visible result of insight is *personal effort* (Nehemiah 8:16–17). A person with insight will put forth whatever effort it takes to obey God.

Can you imagine the ridicule these grown men and women endured from their enemies? The same enemies who had just been defeated in their efforts to stop Israel from building a strong, sturdy wall were now watching even Israel's oldest and wisest, as they gathered sticks and leaves to build huts! No doubt Sanballat and Tobiah were baffled by the people's building habits—and they probably let them know about it, too.

In his book *Enjoying Intimacy with God*, J. Oswald Sanders makes this piercing observation:

> We are at this moment as close to God as we really choose to be. True, there are times when we would like to know a deeper intimacy, but when it comes to the point, we are not prepared to pay the price involved.[5]

The Jews chose to be close to God. And they paid the price with their efforts to make booths according to God's specifications, even when it may have appeared ridiculous to others.

Read Proverbs 2:7–12, and take note of what the Lord promises to do for those who seek wisdom.

_____

_____

_____

The second visible result of insight is *a willingness to change* (Nehemiah 8:16). Those who possess insight are always willing to change according to what they have learned. They choose to leave behind old habits, traditions, and patterns of behavior, seeking instead to live out the truth.

Not just years, but centuries of disobedience had erased this celebration from Israel's memory. Yet despite the pattern of forgetfulness ingrained in the people's hearts, new insight caused "the entire assembly" to welcome a change that would draw them closer to the Lord.

Do old habits, mind-sets, or traditions within your realms of leadership tend to get in the way of your pursuit of godly insight? What are they? How might you break out of these behavioral ruts? Be specific.

_____

_____

_____

The third visible result of insight is *great rejoicing* (Nehemiah 8:17). Those who possess insight are adorned with the joy that comes from being obedient. As inexperienced as they were at celebrating this festival in makeshift booths, and uncomfortable or inconvenient as it must have been, nothing could quench the happiness that flowed from hearts at peace in the shelter of God's will.

> But let all who take refuge in You be glad,
> Let them ever sing for joy;
> And may You shelter them,
> That those who love Your name may exult in You.
> (Psalm 5:11)

Insight leads to immediate obedience, and obedience results in unfathomable joy. Joy doesn't imply ease or a lack of difficulty. It's an unexplainable gift of delight and fulfillment from God.

STARTING YOUR JOURNEY

Like the men and women of Ezra's day, we need more than just occasional insight if we're going to make any real spiritual progress. And just how are we to do that? Consider these two practical suggestions.

First, *we need to spend time in the Scriptures every day* (Nehemiah 8:18). Clothing yourself with the wisdom of God doesn't come from window-shopping in God's Word. You must enter into His storehouse of insights regularly. And when you come across a fitting insight, remember that God's Word is not to be tailored to your life . . . your life must be measured and tailored to fit His Word.

The Message renders Psalm 1:2, "You thrill to [know] God's Word, you chew on Scripture day and night." What words would you use to describe your own feelings or attitude about reading God's Word?

_____

_____

_____

In lesson 10, you were encouraged to select a means to regularly feed on God's Word: hearing, reading, studying, memorizing, or meditating. Have you taken steps to implement this yet? If not, what other priorities are taking precedence? How might you make time in God's Word a priority in the coming days?

_____

_____

_____

_____

If you've kept this commitment, have you noticed any benefits from it? Take a moment to renew your determination before God this next week, making appropriate modifications to your plan as necessary.

_____

_____

_____

_____

Second, *believers need to gather regularly for times of worship and celebration.* Proverbs 27:17 says, "Iron sharpens iron, so one man sharpens another." Ezra pointed the Israelites toward the true source of wisdom and insight, leading them in regular worship and celebration. God intends for believers today to join together in the same way (see Colossians 3:16; Hebrews 10:24–25). We all need the encouragement and strengthening of our faith that come from fellowship with other believers.

Are you consistently attending church and engaging in opportunities for worship and celebration with other believers? If so, how has this helped you sharpen your knowledge and insight? If not, what is keeping you from making this a priority?

_____

_____

_____

_____

Are you content with mere knowledge, or are you looking for something more? Do you honestly yearn for true insight? If so, is your life characterized by effort . . . change . . . and joy? And are you preserving your newfound insight with daily time in God's Word and fellowship with other believers? Insight is a precious gift from God. He intends for us to deeply desire it and to earnestly search for wisdom. And if we seek it with all of our hearts, He has promised that we will find it (see Proverbs 8:17).

LESSON TWELVE

Four Dimensional Praying

Nehemiah 9; 10:29–31, 39

THE HEART OF THE MATTER

After God's people had heard and obeyed His Word by observing the Feast of Tabernacles (Nehemiah 8:13–18), they met for a time of corporate prayer. The celebration brought them to an understanding of both the holiness of God and the depth of their sins, which led to an expression of deep sorrow and humility. Together they prayed, offering up sincere confession as well as thanksgiving and praise. And they committed to change—to study and obey God's commands from that point forward. The Israelites' example provides guidelines for the discipline of prayer that are meaningful, logical, and relevant for us today.

DISCOVERING THE WAY

As the Peanuts cartoon on the following page suggests, superstition and misunderstanding often surround the spiritual discipline of prayer. Many people view prayer as a ceremonial duty, just something one does before meals or at the start of a ballgame. Others treat prayer as a 911 call, deigning to bow their heads only in the direst emergency, when all other options are exhausted. Still others assume that prayer is simply a means of asking God for things. Like Linus in the cartoon, they think that if they could just figure out the magic formula and pray "the right way," then they would be certain to get what they want. And still others—even many Christians—fall somewhere in-between.

The problem is, each of these assumptions completely misses the mark. They ignore the true purpose of prayer and, in doing so, miss out on one of the most precious gifts God has given to His people. God designed prayer as a means of bringing us into an intimate relationship with Himself. Prayer is worth the time and effort it requires; it's our opportunity to spend time with the Creator of the universe!

With the true purpose of prayer in mind, take a few minutes to evaluate the state of your prayer life with this simple quiz.

Are you satisfied with your prayer life?

        Yes   No

Do you always pray with confidence, expecting God to answer?

        Yes   No

When someone asks you to pray for him or her, do you actually do it?

        Yes   No

If you were asked to name four or five specific requests you asked of God this week, could you do that?

        Yes   No

Is your time in the Word of God balanced with meaningful prayer?

        Yes   No

If you could answer yes to all five of these questions, you are free to stop reading now. Your prayer life is in great shape. But if not, you have some room to grow. In Nehemiah 9, we will observe a sincere, heartfelt prayer that provides an excellent model for us today.

OVERVIEW OF THE ISRAELITES' PRAYER

In our previous lesson, the Israelites were faithful to reinstitute the long-forgotten Feast of Tabernacles. On the morning after that memorial celebration, they experienced another unforgettable day of spiritual awakening. To sharpen our understanding and appreciation of the prayer we're about to study, let's pause for a brief overview of three important facts.

First, *this is the longest prayer recorded in the Bible.* It recaps Israel's history, reviewing God's acts of compassion and kindness toward them over the centuries.

 Read Nehemiah 9:1–2.

Second, *the prayer was uttered in a context of humility and purity.* A strange-looking assembly gathered that morning. From every direction a herd of people clad in scraggly goat's hair and with gaunt faces, empty stomachs, grieving hearts, and dirt-covered heads came together and raised their voices as one in an outpouring of confession. The Israelites strongly desired to purge themselves of the sin in their assembly as well as in their hearts.

Had we been there, none of us would have had any difficulty hearing or understanding the confessional cries of the people. But would we have understood the powerful thoughts and emotions spoken in the dialect of fasting, sackcloth, and dirt-covered heads? Let's take a moment to translate. By fasting, they were declaring that their hunger for knowing God was more pressing than the need to satisfy any physical hunger. With their homely, uncomfortable garments of coarse goat's hair, or "sackcloth," they expressed a profound sense of mourning, grief, and humiliation because of their sin and the sins of their forefathers. By throwing dust or ashes on their heads, the people symbolically identified with death and outwardly displayed the feeling of sorrow in the lowest depths of their hearts.[2]

Third, *the prayer reached in four directions.* The Israelites' prayer spanned history from creation to their present day and even looked into the future. First, in Nehemiah 9:5–6, the people looked up in adoration and praise. Second, in 9:7–31, they looked back with heartfelt thanksgiving on all that God had done in their past. Third, in 9:32–37, the people looked around at their present situation and brought a petition before the Lord. And finally, in

9:38, the prayer concluded with a look ahead and a commitment to future obedience.

SPECIFIC EXAMINATION

With this background in mind, let's take a closer look at the structure and purposes of this faith-inspiring prayer, considering each one of its four dimensions.

The first dimension of prayer is *looking up (adoration and praise)*.

 Read Nehemiah 9:5–6.

The Israelites began by praising the "name" of God, which to them was synonymous with the resplendent glory of His being. They praised Him for His exalted position, set on high above the mountains. As they continued, they began to comprehend the grandeur of His peerless sovereignty and praised Him for His matchless creation, which daily heralds His omnipotence, faithfulness, mercy, and love.

In the Scriptures God is known by many names, each of which reveals something different about His character. Look up each Scripture reference below and then meditatively write out all of the thoughts about God's character that this name brings to mind. Next, jot down when you might have felt or seen this particular trait of God in your own life.

Jehovah-Jireh: The LORD Will Provide (Genesis 22:14)

_____

_____

Jehovah-Shalom: The LORD Is Peace (Judges 6:24)

Jehovah-Tsidkenu: The LORD Our Righteousness (Jeremiah 23:6)

Praise gives us perspective by helping us to recognize the reality of who God is and who we are in relation to Him. After the Israelites spent time in verbal adoration, they naturally moved on to a time of reflection, thanking God for what He had done.

The second dimension of prayer is *looking back* (*reflection and thanksgiving*).

 Read Nehemiah 9:7–18.

The lengthiest section of the prayer takes us on a whirlwind tour of Israel's past, documenting the hand of God in each event. As though we are on a journey through the landscape of their history, we see the people's prayer carefully retrace the moral and physical wanderings of their forefathers.

In Nehemiah 9:7–8 we pass through the terrain of Genesis, noting Israel's beginnings, God's promises to Abraham, and God's faithfulness. In

9:9–12, we discover the spectacular signs and wonders of the book of Exodus with the reminder of Israel's captivity under Pharaoh and of God's deliverance. Journeying on, 9:13–15 brings us to the border between Exodus and the meticulously cultivated legal soil of Leviticus, as the people remembered Mount Sinai and the laws governing Jewish life that were given there.

 Read Nehemiah 9:19–31.

Crossing over into Nehemiah 9:19–21, a panoramic view of wilderness wanderings unfolds in a review of the events of Exodus through Deuteronomy. Then, in 9:22–25, suddenly a land of milk and honey appears on the horizon with a brief jaunt through Joshua. From there, we pass through the tall peaks and valleys of the books of Judges, Samuel, Kings, and Chronicles as the Israelites remember the ups and downs of their ancestors' disobedience and God's deliverance (9:26–30).

In the final verse of this section, we see from the hilltop a glimpse of Israel's gracious God in their words: "Nevertheless, in Your great compassion You did not make an end of them or forsake them, / For You are a gracious and compassionate God" (9:31). That is the most beautiful sight of all . . . the one that moved the people from reflection to thanksgiving.

Throughout the Old Testament, one of the key components of Israel's spiritual life involved deliberate reflection upon the works of the Lord and a subsequent time of thanksgiving. The New Testament carries this same theme. Read the following verses.

Philippians 4:6–7

Colossians 4:2

1 Thessalonians 5:18

1 Timothy 2:1

Why do you think thanksgiving is such an important part of our relationship with God?

_____

_____

_____

_____

_____

_____

When was the last time you sat down and deliberately reflected on what God has done in your life? List at least three specific things, and then take time to thank the Lord for each one.

_____

_____

_____

The third dimension of prayer is *looking around (petition and confession)*.

 Read Nehemiah 9:32–37.

In this next section, the Israelites' prayer moved from the past to the present. The people focused again on confession, freely admitting that they were facing hardships because of their sins. And in an impassioned plea, they asked the Lord to enter into the pain they felt as they lived in their own land under the yoke of another nation.

The all-knowing God knew the suffering and pain of the Israelites long before they recognized it themselves. He also understood their needs. However, they still brought their petition to Him, sharing their struggles and pleading

with Him to intercede. The very act of placing their burdens at His feet signi-
fied their faith in His goodness and their submission to His sovereign will.

**If you have a tough time releasing your cares to the Lord, take a few min-
utes to examine the underlying motivations behind your response. Is it
hard for you to believe that God truly cares about your needs? Are you
afraid that His will may involve something that you won't like? Would you
rather trust yourself to handle the issue? Why? Be honest.**

_____

_____

_____

The fourth dimension of prayer is *looking ahead (direction and commitment)*.

 Read Nehemiah 9:38; 10:29–31, 39.

After considering their current situation and presenting their requests to
the Lord, the Israelites began to look toward their future. They remembered
the terrible consequences of disobedience suffered by their forefathers and real-
ized that this would be their future as well if they didn't make a drastic change.

Nehemiah 10 records the names, one by one, of those who stepped up
that day and signed on the dotted line of the covenant. The specific provi-
sions of the agreement are also recorded there. The people agreed to "walk in
God's law, which was given through Moses, God's servant, and to keep and
to observe all the commandments of GOD" (Nehemiah 10:29). The essence
of their commitment could be distilled into one word—*obedience*.

STARTING YOUR JOURNEY

The Israelites' prayer led to obedience. The process of recognizing God's greatness through praise and reflecting on His provision with thankfulness is designed to lead us to a realization of our own sinfulness, dependence on Him, and a deep commitment to change.

Consider the four dimensions of prayer: praise, thanksgiving, petition, and commitment. Choose one, and write out a specific plan for incorporating it into your life this week. (For example, first thing each morning, take a few minutes to praise God for being who He is.)

_____

_____

_____

Now consider your realm of leadership, and choose a dimension of prayer to practice with those around you. (For example, change a mealtime prayer to a more significant prayer by planning a time of reflection at the table with your family or friends.) Outline your plan here.

_____

_____

_____

_____

The purpose behind the Israelites' prayer was far more than a time of praise and thanksgiving, though those are worthy pursuits. It even moved beyond sincere petition, also a key element of the discipline of prayer. Ultimately, it set forth a solemn agreement between the people and their God. And it should serve the same purpose in our lives today, moving us from adoration and thanksgiving to obedience.

LESSON THIRTEEN

Putting First Things First

Nehemiah 10

THE HEART OF THE MATTER

In Nehemiah's day, when the people of Jerusalem prayed, they meant business! They did not offer mere words—they signed their names to a sealed document (Nehemiah 9:38). The document contained an agreement that was prepared and established before God. In it they promised to pattern their lives according to His truth, to put first things first. In this lesson, we'll carefully examine this promise, recognizing the impact of our priorities on our lives.

DISCOVERING THE WAY

In an interview several years ago, a very successful industrialist was asked: in all his dealings with people, what was the most difficult thing to get them to do? After brief reflection, he named two things, in the order of their importance. The first and most difficult is encouraging people to think before they act. The second is persuading people to maintain proper priorities, to do things in the order of their importance.

The book of Nehemiah provides a powerful testimony to the importance of preceding any decision with careful thought and then following through with decisive action. For instance, at the beginning of the story, when Nehemiah heard that the wall was still down and the people were in distress, he didn't grab a trowel and head for Jerusalem. He spent four months thinking and praying about the problem before he acted. And later, when opposition came, he controlled his knee-jerk inclination to retaliate and took time to plan the best way to respond.

Similarly, when the time came to reorganize their government according to God's commands, Israel didn't plunge into the task with blind zeal. They first spent time regaining their spiritual vision through thinking and meditating on God's Law (Nehemiah 9).

All of these factors led to a decision—a right decision to reverse the wrong priorities that had come from foolish thinking and selfish choices in the past. With the last verse in Nehemiah 9, the people determined to establish an agreement with God based on new priorities.

Make a list of your top five personal priorities as a believer:

1. _____

2. _____

3. _____

4. _____

5. _____

Do the time and energy you spend on each of these areas reflect their importance to you? Why, or why not?

_____

_____

_____

THE DOCUMENT OF PROMISE

On July 2, 1776, a group of American colonists known as the Continental Congress voted to ratify the contents of one of our nation's most cherished documents—the Declaration of Independence. In Nehemiah 10, Israel conducted a "continental congress" of their own as the nation's leaders stepped up to sign their names to a vitally important document—a declaration of dependence on God.

This document of promise served as an official contract between the people and the Lord, reestablishing right priorities built on His laws. Nehemiah 10:29 uses two specific words to describe the contract: "a curse and an oath." Inherent in the word for *curse* is the idea of coming into an oath with God that, if it is broken, allows the consequences of a curse. In light of the seriousness with which the revived remnant of Israel viewed God's Word, we can be confident that they took their written oath with the utmost reverence.

GETTING TO THE ROOT
The Depth of an Oath

In Nehemiah 10:29 the people took on themselves "a curse and an oath" to follow God's ways. The Hebrew word *shava*, "to swear an oath," is a vivid term that stems from a root that means "to seven oneself" or "bind oneself by seven things."[1] In the ancient world, the Hebrews didn't seal a contract or an oath with a mere handshake or a signature on a piece of papyrus. Instead, they literally did seven things related to their oath as a way of binding themselves to the promise. We're not told what the seven things were in this case, but we find other examples in the Bible. For example, when Abraham made an oath to King Abimelech, he gave the king seven ewe lambs (see Genesis 21:28–32). These lambs served as living reminders of Abraham's oath.

THE PEOPLE OF THE PROMISE

 Skim Nehemiah 10:1–28.

Those who signed the declaration of dependence on God numbered eighty-four. Following Nehemiah's signature were the names of twenty-two priests (Nehemiah 10:1–8), seventeen Levites (10:9–13), and forty-four leaders of the people (10:14–27).

According to Nehemiah 10:28, the people who committed themselves to the task of obedience had two things in common. First, they physically removed themselves from the pagan influence of foreigners—they "separated themselves from the peoples of the lands to the law of God." And second, they were old enough to understand the contents of the document. But that doesn't mean they were all male dignitaries or elders in the community! Also included were "their wives, their sons and their daughters, all those who had knowledge and understanding" (Nehemiah 10:28).

THE IMPORTANCE OF THE DOCUMENT

Just like the American colonists, Israel needed a rallying point, a unifying formal declaration telling friends and enemies alike of their decision to change their ways, to be distinct from those around them. America's Declaration of Independence was the birth certificate of a brand-new nation. Israel's declaration of dependence became the birth certificate of a spiritually reborn nation.

Consider your realms of leadership. Have you ever "officially" published the group's priorities in the form of a purpose or vision statement or goals? How? To whom?

_____

_____

_____

_____

What benefit would such a statement of values, purpose, goals, or strategies have on those within your realms of leadership?

_____

_____

_____

THE PROMISES IN THE DOCUMENT

Now let's look inside the document at the promises themselves, both general and specific. Israel knew what many Americans have forgotten—that life, liberty, and the pursuit of happiness all rest on our relationship with God. And so the general theme behind Israel's document was one of obedience to His written Word—in their case, the Law of Moses.

 Read Nehemiah 10:28–29.

The Jews' promise of obedience included an official declaration of secession. They separated themselves from a world that followed the whims of the latest philosophies and pagan religions (Nehemiah 10:28). In order to do this, Israel had to resist the powerful pull of the culture around them, even if it meant facing ridicule and rejection. Israel was willing to stand alone in obedience to the Lord. By patterning their lives after the Law of Moses, they would be God pleasers rather than people pleasers.

Do you find yourself being a people pleaser, preferring to make others happy, satisfied, or impressed rather than taking a stand? Are there certain people or situations within your realms of leadership that make this harder than others? Explain your perspective.

_____

_____

_____

How can careful, clear priorities help prevent you and those you lead from succumbing to peer pressure?

_____

_____

Following their general declaration of dependence upon the Lord, Israel then clarified the details of their promise to obey in three important areas: home, society, and place of worship.

 Read Nehemiah 10:30.

First, the Israelites promised to keep their home and family relationships clear of foreign influence. From experience, they knew that their Achilles'

heel was their tendency to intermarry with people from pagan lands. The exchange of sons and daughters led to the exchange of religions, eventually diluting Israel's faith in God.

One painful memory that may have prompted Israel's promise is found in Judges 3. God had led the Jews out of slavery in Egypt. Just prior to entering the Promised Land, Moses told the people that this land flowing with milk and honey also contained a forbidden fruit. No Israelite was to choose a wife for himself from among the pagan nations or to give his daughter away to a foreigner. But once they settled in the land, the new residents couldn't resist the fruit's lure, and their disobedience plunged the nation back into bondage (Judges 3:5–8).

Though New Testament believers are never forbidden from marrying people of different backgrounds or nationalities, we are warned against close partnerships with unbelievers (2 Corinthians 6:14). This warning covers marriage to unbelievers, close business relationships, and other close partnerships.

Read 2 Corinthians 6:14–17. How might close partnerships or business relationships with unbelievers distract you from your priorities as a believer?

_____

_____

_____

_____

 Read Nehemiah 10:31.

With the second specific promise, the people of Israel extended their obedience from their homes into their society. They committed to restore the weekly and yearly calendars that governed Israel's life. By refusing to buy goods on the Sabbath and through other practices, they would carry their faith and distinctiveness into the marketplace and their world. According to one author, this kind of visible difference is sorely missing in many Christians' lives today.

It has never ceased to amaze me that we Christians have developed a kind of selective vision which allows us to be deeply and sincerely involved in worship and church activities and yet almost totally pagan in the day-in, day-out guts of our business lives . . . and never realize it.[2]

List below nonverbal ways that Christian-led businesses and organizations convey to the world that God is their top priority. Include things they refuse to do as well as things they do.

_____

_____

_____

_____

_____

Which of these do you encourage within your realms of leadership? What does this reflect about your priorities in your private and public life?

_____

_____

_____

_____

_____

Read Nehemiah 10:32–39.

In Nehemiah 10:32–39, the house of God—Israel's place of worship—is mentioned nine times. Verse 39 sums up the promises of the people regarding their worship: "Thus we will not neglect the house of our God." By donating a portion of their income, the tithe (Numbers 18:21), they would fund the ministry of the temple so that the priests could again offer sacrifices for the people. Following the laws commanded by God in the past, the people again committed to dedicate to God the "first fruits"—their firstborn sons and animals (Exodus 13:2), the first of their crops (Exodus 23:19; 34:26), and the first of their dough (Leviticus 23:17). In so doing, they would reinstitute worship of God at the temple. It would be a top priority.

At this time in Israel's history, the temple was literally the dwelling place of God. Today, however, God does not reside in a building made with human hands. In 1 Corinthians 6:19, Paul gave us God's new address: "Do you not know that your body is a temple of the Holy Spirit who is in you, whom you have from God, and that you are not your own?"

As believers, we are privileged to have the presence of the Lord in the temple of our bodies. Therefore, wherever we go, whatever we say, and whatever we think or do, we should do it all as unto the Lord (1 Corinthians 10:31). And we should order our priorities accordingly.

 STARTING YOUR JOURNEY

Our own lives can be living documents of obedience to our Lord, but to do so, we must heed three principles from our lesson.

First, *serious thought precedes any significant change.* You cannot waste time dabbling in shallow thinking and careless priorities without diminishing who you could be and what you might do in the future. In other words, change is dependent upon the planning that precedes it.

Reexamine the five personal priorities you listed at the beginning of this lesson. How much time and thought did you put into them? On what did you base these priorities? Would you consider them well-planned?

How closely do your realms of leadership reflect carefully thought-out, godly priorities?

Second, *written plans confirm right priorities.* Most of us are not used to writing our priorities on paper. Typically we keep them like children's toys in a mental chest full of ideas all jumbled together. Disentangling them from the frivolous, the unrelated, and the outdated requires writing them down, straightening them out on paper. Otherwise, all those impressive priorities we carry around in our heads and occasionally discuss with others will simply remain mental and never become life-changing catalysts.

In light of this lesson, would you revise your list of personal priorities or those of your business or group? If so, schedule some time this week when you can thoughtfully and prayerfully reconsider them. You may wish to write down supporting Bible verses and other thoughts in a journal. Jot down your new list below.

_____

_____

_____

_____

If a document like the one signed by the Israelites were drawn up today, publicly declaring faith in the Lord Jesus Christ as top priority and plans to follow His Word in all areas of your life, would you sign it?

Third, *loss of distinction and conformity to the world go hand in hand.* Apart from your attendance at Bible studies and church, can anyone look at you and recognize the distinctiveness of Christianity? Look at your home, your work, your relationships, and ask yourself, "Am I really any different from the world?"

If somebody were to examine your priorities, would they see them as different from the world's priorities and pursuits? How do they differ? How are they the same?

_____

_____

_____

_____

_____

Under Nehemiah's leadership and Ezra's teaching, the people of Israel put first things first—their devotion to God, their relationships with their families, their distinctiveness in society, and their spiritual lives took precedence over all else. Their devotion to God's Word meant a reordering of their priorities without a contradiction between what they believed and what they lived. The same is true for us today. Only after careful reflection regarding our personal and public priorities in line with God's desires for us can we have complete confidence in our pursuits.

LESSON FOURTEEN

The Willing Unknowns

Nehemiah 7:1–4; 11

THE HEART OF THE MATTER

Tucked away in the Bible are verses that seldom, if ever, attract the attention of the hurried reader. Because our pace is so often accelerated, we miss many of the hidden treasures God has stored up for us in His Word. In this lesson, we'll uncover one such treasure. Nehemiah 11 recognizes the "willing unknowns," a special group of people who served a vital function in Jerusalem but never saw their names in lights. In this lesson, we will consider our own sacrificial service and learn to appreciate those who work behind the scenes in our home, workplace, and realm of leadership.

DISCOVERING THE WAY

Do these names ring a bell? Charlotte Elliott . . . Stuart K. Hine . . . Edward Perronet . . . Thomas O. Chisholm. You may have seen these names before and forgotten them. But if you grew up in a traditional church, you probably know their words by heart: "Just as I Am" . . .

"How Great Thou Art" . . . "All Hail the Power of Jesus' Name" . . . "Great Is Thy Faithfulness." Unlike some of the more renowned hymn writers, these and countless others are part of God's "willing unknowns." Though their names never lit up Broadway or filled chapters of history books, their faithful ministries of music continue to affect us today.

In fact, throughout the ages God's work has been accomplished not only by a few heroes of the faith, but also by the many hands of the faithful. Have you ever heard of Athaiah, the son of Uzziah? Or Gabbai and Sallai? How about Maaseiah, the son of Baruch? It's doubtful; Scripture mentions them only once in a long list of unpronounceable names in Nehemiah 11. Yet each one played a crucial role in the success of Nehemiah's project—reestablishing the city of Jerusalem.

Who would you say have been the most dependable people in your life, who have faithfully and humbly carried out their roles without pursuing their own glory or complaining that they don't get recognition? Try to list at least three names, either within your realms of leadership or in other areas of your life.

_____

_____

_____

_____

How would your relationships or projects suffer without the contributions of each of these people? What unique gifts, skills, or perspectives does each one contribute?

_____

_____

_____

_____

_____

HISTORICAL BACKGROUND

You may have noticed that we skipped Nehemiah 7 earlier in our study of the book of Nehemiah. That omission wasn't accidental. Nehemiah 7 serves best as a backdrop to Nehemiah 11.

 Read Nehemiah 7:1–4.

At the beginning of Nehemiah 7, the wall around Jerusalem had just been completed, security established, responsibility delegated, and the daily schedule set (7:1–3).

Part of Nehemiah's task in restoring the city's wall was to help revive the city itself. To a Jew, Jerusalem was a place of great honor—"The City of David," their promised inheritance, and the dwelling place of their God. So once the wall was in place, Nehemiah's next task was to bring back God's people to live inside.

 Read Nehemiah 11:1–2.

Casting lots was like rolling dice. Though it sounds rather arbitrary and random, it was one of the ways God led His people in making decisions throughout the Bible (see Leviticus 16:8; Joshua 18:6–10; 1 Chronicles 24:31). As the Israelites went through this process, God selected one-tenth of the people to move into the city (Nehemiah 11:1).

God also worked in the hearts of some who hadn't been chosen by lot (Nehemiah 11:2). They volunteered! This group is the first of the willing unknowns memorialized in this story. The word translated as "volunteered" comes from the Hebrew word *nadab*, which implies the idea of generosity and willingness.[1] Exodus 35 illustrates this concept when it describes the people of Israel who constructed the tabernacle. Those silent servants skilled in craftsmanship, embroidery, weaving, and other arts gave of their treasures, talents, and time for the service of God. Yet not one name from that group of volunteers is recorded or remembered. In the same way, the volunteers of Nehemiah 11 uprooted their families, packed their belongings, and built new homes on land covered with tumbled-down structures likely overgrown with weeds and overrun with vermin.

Take a moment to imagine the extremely difficult circumstances these volunteers faced as they packed their things and moved their families out of their comfort zones into the rough unknown—permanently. Read Psalm 48:1–3, 8–14. What motivated these people to make a sacrifice?

_____

_____

_____

_____

Think about the behind-the-scenes people you listed earlier. What do you think is the motivation behind their sacrificial service? What characteristics do they have in common with the Israelite volunteers?

_____

_____

_____

_____

Do you serve as a willing unknown in any area of your life (church, work-place, community, or school)? Where? Would you be content if you remained unacknowledged in that role for the rest of your life? Why, or why not?

_____

_____

_____

_____

Read Colossians 3:23–24. How does this passage address our attitude toward the tasks we've been given? What should be our motivation? What do you find most challenging about applying this passage?

_____

_____

_____

_____

THE WILLING UNKNOWNS IN NEHEMIAH 11

Groups of willing unknowns fill the text of Nehemiah 11. We've already noticed the first group, *the people who volunteered to move.* We find the second group when we glance down at 11:10–12.

 Read Nehemiah 11:10–12.

The *people who worked within the temple* numbered eight hundred and twenty-two—that's quite a ministry staff! And not one of them was named. We can bet that a good percentage did jobs that most people took for grant-ed, like dusting, lighting lamps, and cleaning up after the "big-wigs" like

Jedaiah and Seraiah, whose names actually made it into the Bible. These folks served anonymously so that God's people would be blessed as they came to worship.

 Read Nehemiah 11:15–16.

The next group of willing unknowns included *those who worked outside the place of worship.* The phrase "in charge of the outside work" refers to two types of tasks: maintaining the exterior of the temple and its grounds and serving people in areas such as judging and counseling.

 Read Nehemiah 11:17.

The fourth group consisted of *those who supported the ministry through prayer.* Have you ever seen a best seller titled *The Prayer of Mattaniah*? Of course not. That prayer warrior's fervent words on his knees went unnoticed by men . . . but not by the almighty God. Mattaniah, Bakbukiah, and Abda probably didn't preach, landscape, or clean, but they prayed with all their might to keep the temple ministry alive.

 Read Nehemiah 11:22–23.

The final group of willing unknowns included *those who served the Lord with singing.* This was no last-minute quartet, but a group of committed musicians who willingly developed their gifts and gave their time on behalf of the people and to the praise of God. This unnumbered and unnamed choir faithfully carried out its task with excellence day after day.

As you review the five groups of willing unknowns described in Nehemiah 11, consider some of the unsung accomplishments and daily tasks that you may not usually notice as you focus on more high-profile people and projects. Can you give names of volunteers, support staff, maintenance crewmembers, prayer supporters, or other "behind-the-scenes" servants? If so, list them below.

_____

_____

_____

_____

_____

If you don't know the names of these people, what valuable but low-profile tasks come to mind that you may not have noticed before, but through this lesson have now recognized as important?

_____

_____

_____

What are some examples of similar tasks or acts of service that you provide to others?

_____

_____

_____

PRACTICAL PRINCIPLES FOR TODAY

Why spend a whole lesson studying a bunch of people nobody ever heard of, whose names we'll never remember? At times we all struggle with our self-esteem or self-worth. Every one of us occasionally wonders if we make any difference at all, or we question the value of our gifts and talents. But even if you haven't wondered yourself, you can be sure the willing unknowns under your leadership have pondered these issues during moments of discouragement. This unpronounceable passage of Scripture gives us three helpful principles that can encourage us during these times of self-doubt.

First, *your gift makes you valuable, if not necessarily popular.* Being a leader can be a lonely, often thankless job. Sometimes there is little room for failure or mistakes. And others may not notice or understand the extra time and energy you devote to your role. But God sees, and He knows your heart. The same is true of those who are gifted in an area that never reaches the spotlight. They are as valuable as Mattaniah or Uzzi and just as well-known to God.

Second, *every labor done in love is remembered by God, never forgotten.* Hebrews 6:10 says, "For God is not unjust so as to forget your work and the love which you have shown toward His name, in having ministered and in still ministering to the saints." This applies to your most public duties as well as your most private actions. Even if nobody notices your faithfulness, God does. So be faithful!

Third, *our final reward in heaven will be determined on the basis of personal faithfulness, not public applause.* The public may never know of your ministry, whether it takes place in the privacy of your prayer closet or on the back row of the choir. God will reward you in heaven based on the pure-hearted service of your life, rather than according to the number of plaques, trophies, or thank-you notes you've received.

Paul wrote, "For by grace you have been saved through faith; and that not of yourselves, it is the gift of God; not as a result of works, so that no one may boast" (Ephesians 2:8–9). Whether you go to heaven or not has nothing to do with your accomplishments on earth. Heaven is a free gift. To learn more about this, read "How to Begin a Relationship with God" at the back of this book.

STARTING YOUR JOURNEY

Applying these principles requires a genuine attitude of *humility*. As servants, ministers, or employees, it takes a humble heart and willing hands to be faithful day-in and day-out without any expectation of recognition, applause, or reward. On the other hand, leaders and employers should also not underestimate the confidence and encouragement that results when those who work under their leadership are recognized for their faithfulness.

Spend some time over the next several days meditating on the following two passages of Scripture. What do they say about your significance in God's kingdom? About the significance of those within your realms of leadership?

Mark 10:42–45

_____

_____

_____

1 Corinthians 12:4–26

_____

_____

_____

If you are not involved in serving as a willing unknown, think of a specific task that needs volunteers, either at your church, in your community, or at your workplace. Set aside your pride or personal preferences and commit to using your time, energy, or skills to help meet this need. How will you begin?

_____

_____

There may be several unknown but valuable names within your sphere of influence. This lesson may have already surfaced some of them you've overlooked—the person who cleans your workspace, the maintenance man who controls the temperature, those who care for or teach your children, or the choir members who lead in worship every Sunday. Realizing that it's easy for willing unknowns to get discouraged from time to time, why not drop a note in the mail or speak a thank-you to them?

In the next few days, what specifically will you do to show your appreciation for the faithfulness of workers or team members who often go unnoticed?

_____

_____

_____

_____

Willing unknowns are everywhere. In fact, one could make the argument that without the many hands that make things happen, leaders would be nothing but talking heads spouting empty words. Scripture is filled with examples of unnamed faithful servants who often spend their whole lives without recognition or reward. At the same time, we are called to encourage one another through kind words of appreciation. In light of the example of these unsung heroes, be content with your own quiet work, but also be complimentary of the quiet work of others.

LESSON FIFTEEN

Happiness Is on the Wall

Nehemiah 12:27–47

THE HEART OF THE MATTER

Chapter after chapter of Nehemiah is filled with challenges, setbacks, criticism, and sorrow as the returning Jews rebuilt the wall around Jerusalem. But Nehemiah 12 marks a dramatic change. Following the completion of their immense task, the Jews responded with joy—intense happiness. The city overflowed with the sound of singing. Instruments of music blended with the celebration scene as the triumphant tone of rejoicing was heard from afar (Nehemiah 12:43). In this uplifting lesson, we'll attempt to recreate that happy scene in our minds and glean from it several practical lessons about joy and celebration of God's mighty works.

DISCOVERING THE WAY

In November of 1989, while Americans prepared to celebrate Thanksgiving, East Germans were celebrating their own unforgettable moment of thanksgiving. The wall that had for so long kept them incarcerated in a communist regime was finally coming down. The power of the old party leaders had begun to crumble. Along with that ruling power tumbled its symbol—the Berlin Wall—almost as quickly and unexpectedly as it had been raised in August 1961. Amidst the rubble, people erupted with cheering, dancing, singing, crying, and hugging in celebration.

A festive scene similar to this twentieth-century event occurred thousands of years ago in Nehemiah's day. But on that occasion, the celebration centered on a wall being raised up, not torn down. The Israelites, too, rejoiced with exuberant singing, dancing, and celebration, their physical expression echoing the emotion in their hearts.

If people examined your words, attitudes, and actions, would they believe you're a happy or joyous person? Why, or why not?

_____

_____

Would their conclusion accurately reflect how you actually feel? Explain.

_____

_____

DEDICATION OF THE WALL

Behind Jerusalem's broad, well-constructed wall, a renewed vision brought fresh signs of growth to a barren city. Commerce began to bud again, homes sprouted up, and an influx of new people brought a healthy glow to a city awakening from a long night's sleep. In Nehemiah 12:27, Nehemiah resumed the movement of his narrative with a description of the preparations for the dedication ceremony.

Read Nehemiah 12:27–30.

In order for Nehemiah and Ezra to accomplish the planned celebration, they needed the help of the Levites, a special tribe in Israel responsible for leading worship. But recruiting these men was not a simple matter of making a few phone calls or e-mailing a few meeting requests. According to Nehemiah 11:18, the task consisted of contacting two hundred and eighty-four men in Jerusalem . . . besides all those who still lived outside the city walls (12:28–29). Why was it necessary to reach those specific men? They were the descendants of Levi, specialists in temple and tabernacle activities. And if the wall was to be dedicated for the glory of God, the Levites needed to plan and lead the celebration.

According to Nehemiah 12:27, in what manner were the Levites to celebrate the dedication? Describe the mood of this event in your own words.

_____

_____

_____

_____

Before the celebration began, time was set aside for purification (Nehemiah 12:30). How did they purify themselves? We're not privy to exact details, but more than likely the priests and Levites made "sin offerings" on behalf of the people. The ceremonial sacrifice of animals was a practice instituted by God as a means for His people to be cleansed from sin. He also appointed offerings of grain, animals, produce, and other goods to be made for the purposes of worship and thanksgiving, as we'll see in the next section. Before the celebration of the wall could begin, before it could be enjoyed without reservation, the people's hearts needed to be pure, cleansed by the confession of sin.

How might unconfessed sin hinder a person's joy and celebration?

_____

_____

_____

Because of the advent of Jesus Christ, New Testament believers do not offer animal sacrifices as the Old Testament worshipers did. Instead, we are exhorted to offer other types of sacrifices as part of our celebration of God and His mighty works. Read each of the following passages, and in your own words describe the types of sacrifices believers may offer today.

Romans 12:1–2

_____

_____

Hebrews 13:15

_____

_____

1 Peter 2:5

_____

_____

Is your own sacrifice of joy and praise being hindered by unconfessed sin or guilt? If so, study David's words of repentance in Psalm 51. Note at least three insights you discover regarding confession and repentance. Then, spend some time in prayer, seeking forgiveness and purification from the Lord.

_____

_____

_____

_____

_____

Next, Nehemiah recorded the details of his preparation for the celebration.

 Read Nehemiah 12:31–43.

Imagine dozens, perhaps even hundreds, of singers and musicians clambering onto the new wall, grouping themselves together for last-minute vocal and instrumental tuning as the celebration started! Finally, the bands began to play, the choirs sang, and Ezra and Nehemiah set off in opposite directions along the sturdy wall, rejoicing and trampling underfoot the scoffing of their enemies.

When these divided troupes met back together in the temple court, joy reigned. The Israelites cheerfully offered sacrifices, and "even the women and children rejoiced, so that the joy of Jerusalem was heard from afar" (Nehemiah 12:43).

DEDICATION OF THE PEOPLE

Besides dedicating the wall to the Lord that day, the people also committed themselves to supporting the priests and the Levites financially and to living consecrated lives.

 Read Nehemiah 12:44–47.

In this description of the dedication of the people, it's clear that their joyous celebration and sacrifices transformed them personally. The prevailing spirit of joy encouraged the people to give gladly to the needs of those appointed to oversee the temple (Nehemiah 12:44, 47). Also, they consecrated their lives, committing to keep the Law of Moses. In this way, the ceremony contained a balance of truth and emotion, words and song, and a healthy respect for the ancient traditions of their forefathers (12:45–46).

In addition to singing and maintaining a positive attitude, joy is also expressed through cheerful generosity. Joy affects our attitude toward things we tend to hold on to, such as money and time. Delightfully giving those things away is the *result* of joy as well as often being a *stimulus* for it. When you delight in the Lord, you desire to give to others; when you give to others, you receive joyful satisfaction. They go hand in hand.

Read 2 Corinthians 9:6–7. Is your public life characterized by cheerful giving of your money and your time? Is your private life?

_____

_____

_____

_____

_____

_____

_____

STARTING YOUR JOURNEY

No one who saw or heard the boisterous cheers and praises of the Israelites that day would have had any doubts about the vibrancy of their faith. Let's take a moment to examine the vitality of our own faith according to these four solid, applicable principles.

First, recognize that *an atmosphere of happiness should surround God's people.* One of the most magnetic and powerful forces in any ministry or leadership is the presence of joy. Do you contribute to an atmosphere of joy or detract from it? Do you genuinely enjoy getting together with other believers to offer up praise in song and through giving? Are you enjoyable to be around, or do you give off signals that you'd rather not be bothered by people? An atmosphere of joy should be easily apparent when Christians gather together.

Based on your own study of the following passages, describe the relationship between joy and the Christian life. Consider some of these questions: Where does joy come from? What are its effects? Is it an option or a necessity? A feeling or a choice? What things can take joy away from you? How and when should joy be expressed? You may want to spend some of your daily devotional time in this exercise.

Psalm 16:11; 21:6; 92:4
Galatians 5:22
Proverbs 15:13, 15
1 Thessalonians 2:19–20

_____

_____

_____

_____

_____

Read Nehemiah 12:46 and 1 Thessalonians 5:16–18. What do you think is the relationship between having joy, praying, and giving thanks?

_____

_____

_____

Next, realize that *music is one of the most expressive ways to communicate joy.* You would be hard-pressed to find a genuinely happy Christian who doesn't enjoy either participating in or listening to music. Music has been given by God to enhance the joy of a worship service and inspire the hearts of Christians. It is one of the most expressive ways we can communicate happiness. Why? Because "music short-circuits the senses with a direct pathway into human emotion."[1] Whether we play an instrument, harmonize in the choir, sing in the shower, or whistle a tune to our children or grandkids, music tends to flow from us when we have joy in our hearts.

DIGGING DEEPER
Music and Learning

Besides serving as both a cause and effect of joy, music is also a powerful tool for teaching and memorization. Music, particularly singing, is one of the few activities that engages both sides of the brain. This interaction between the right and left brain allows for quicker transmission of information from short-term memory to long-term memory. In fact, research indicates that music activates a variety of memory systems, including "listening, attention, concentration, and recall."[2]

Therefore, music is an excellent way to teach truth. The Israelites used this method to transfer vital truths about their God and their history to successive generations. These "hymns of heritage" sustained their identity and unity as a people (see Psalm 44 and 66 for examples).

And consider the numerous hymns, choruses, creeds, and psalms that permeate more recent church history. Music has been the primary tool used to teach doctrinal truth to generations of Christians. Paul exhorted believers in Ephesians 5:19, "[speak] to one another in psalms and hymns and spiritual songs." Music is still an integral part of today's worship.

According to Ephesians 5:18–20 and Colossians 3:16, what purposes besides expressing joy does music serve for believers? What is the source of this music?

_____

_____

_____

In light of the spiritual benefits of worshiping or learning through music, how can you incorporate it into your life this week? Be specific.

_____

_____

_____

_____

Next, remember that *a joyful spirit will have far-reaching effects.* What was it that was "heard from afar" (Nehemiah 12:43) when the great choirs sang atop the walls? Not the singing, not the instruments, but "the joy of Jerusalem" (12:43). Even for all the money and equipment spent and used today to deliver the Christian message, no television station, radio tower, or Internet connection can match the magnetic power of Christians exhibiting God's joy on a day-to-day basis.

When you visit a church, business, or other organization, how does a joyful spirit among the people there affect you as a visitor? Contrast this positive impact with the atmosphere of places where the people have negative or sour attitudes.

_____

_____

_____

Briefly analyze the "joy level" in your realm of responsibility. As a leader, how can you positively influence those within your realm of leadership by demonstrating joyful attitudes and actions? Suggest several specific actions you might take to deliberately cultivate an atmosphere of joy and light-heartedness.

_____

_____

_____

_____

Finally, recognize that *joy is not dependent upon outward circumstances but upon inward focus.* If you doubt this, look at the circumstances surrounding the Israelites before, during, and after their celebration. They were still under Persian authority, living in a city filled with rubble, and they were unceasingly hounded by outside enemies who opposed them. But they celebrated with a joy that practically shook the homes of their critics. Why? Because they focused completely on the Almighty God. Our circumstances don't determine whether or not we experience or express joy in the Lord. Regardless of what the world may lead us to believe, happiness is a heart matter.

What circumstances today are robbing you of your joy?

_____

_____

_____

_____

_____

Read Isaiah's account of the Messiah's ministry in Isaiah 61:1–3. In Jesus's name and by the power of the Holy Spirit, ask God to exchange your mourning for the oil of gladness, to give you peace and joy in the midst of your troublesome circumstances. Take a few moments to write out your prayer here.

_____

_____

_____

_____

According to Nehemiah 12:43, "The joy of Jerusalem was heard from afar." Regardless of trying circumstances, Nehemiah and the people of Jerusalem celebrated with joyful song and generosity the work God had done through them. We must not underestimate the power of joy for the believer. The secret of happiness is daily, moment-by-moment trusting in the sovereign God of heaven. As a child of God, you have reason to celebrate . . . so rejoice and sing!

LESSON SIXTEEN

Taking Problems by the Throat

Nehemiah 13

 THE HEART OF THE MATTER

One of the occupational hazards of leadership is the need to face, analyze, and solve problems. While supervising the construction of the wall and later while governing the people of Jerusalem, Nehemiah faced and wisely dealt with many knotty, complicated problems. In this final lesson, we will observe Nehemiah as he addressed four critical problems. From his example, we will draw several timely, applicable principles for our own realms of leadership.

 DISCOVERING THE WAY

Ludwig van Beethoven has been described as the "musician who felt, thought, and dreamt in tones."[1] By the end of his life he had written nine symphonies, five concertos, and countless minuets, chamber pieces, and sonatas.

In contrast to the great heights of his professional success, Beethoven's personal life was marked with many problems and setbacks. As an adult, Beethoven lived with a catastrophic irony—the loss of his hearing.

Yet Beethoven channeled his intense anger and frustration over his deafness into an indomitable determination to continue composing, which was summed up by his words, "I will take Fate by the throat."[2] The louder the silence roared in his ears, the more richly and intensely the music flowed from his heart. In fact, the moving notes of his legendary Ninth Symphony flowed from an inner world of silence.

Like Beethoven, Nehemiah refused to let problems conquer him. Intensely desiring to please the Lord, Nehemiah took sin "by the throat" wherever he found it. Throughout our study we have seen him ward off enemies and stir up a glorious spirit of revival among his people. But nowhere is his indomitable spirit more obvious than in his response to the four serious problems recorded in Nehemiah 13.

If you were to name the most difficult, complicated problem you're facing today that affects your realms of leadership, what would it be? Why is it so difficult?

_____

_____

How have you responded to this problem? Have you avoided it, hoping it would work itself out, or have you been waging a war against it to no avail?

_____

_____

Describe how this problem affects you personally. Does it annoy you, weary you, or anger you? Why?

_____

_____

_____

_____

PROBLEMS IN NEHEMIAH'S DAY

Nehemiah's time in Jerusalem was amazingly fruitful, but he was honor-bound to return to his former position as cupbearer to King Artaxerxes (Nehemiah 2:6). We don't know exactly how long he was away from Jerusalem before asking permission to return (13:6). However, it was long enough for the children of Israel to get themselves into some serious trouble—the kind of trouble that could eventually deafen the ears of the whole nation to the words of the Lord. Though they were once eager to listen and obey (13:1–3), their eagerness waned, leading to several problems Nehemiah had to face upon his return.

The first problem Nehemiah encountered was a *compromising companionship*.

 Read Nehemiah 13:4–9.

An Israelite priest, Eliashib, offered part of the temple as a private hotel suite for one of Jerusalem's worst enemies: Tobiah. You may recall that Tobiah had been an opponent of the rebuilding project from the beginning. Yet while Nehemiah was away, this man wormed his way not just behind the walls of the city, but inside the sacred walls of the temple. And the high priest allowed it.

When Nehemiah returned and discovered what had taken place, he stormed through the temple and did some long-overdue house cleaning

(Nehemiah 13:7–9). Nehemiah's response was godly, swift, and decisive. He righteously corrected the wrong. Some people undoubtedly thought that Nehemiah was overreacting or being unreasonable. But fortunately for Israel, Nehemiah wasn't interested in winning any popularity contests. His only interest was in cleaning out the evil that had already affected the people's ability to hear and obey the Word of the Lord. The coddling of their enemy had led to a compromising of integrity.

Had Nehemiah been in Jerusalem, Tobiah never would have been allowed to weasel his way in. Yet few leaders today have that excuse. Many problems fester right under a leader's nose or behind his or her back. When the problem eventually explodes, the solution is more traumatic and the recovery takes much longer than it would have if it had been handled early and swiftly.

Scripture exhorts us to be alert to problems and to handle them as soon as they arise. How does each of the following passages support the principle of keeping short accounts of problems?

1 Samuel 3:11–14

_____

_____

Proverbs 24:30–34

_____

_____

Matthew 18:15–17

_____

_____

1 Corinthians 5:1–13

_____

_____

In your experience, what are the usual results of neglecting problems?

_____

_____

Next, Nehemiah dealt with a *financial fiasco.*

Read Nehemiah 13:10–14.

Nehemiah didn't have to look very long before he came across financial waywardness (Nehemiah 13:10). According to the Law of Moses, the Levites were assigned to minister in and around the temple, and the people were commanded to support them financially through the practice of tithing. But because the tithes had ceased to be distributed, the Levites had been forced to go back to their farms to make a living. Nehemiah cleaned house, appointing reliable accountants to make sure the finances flowed properly (13:11–14). Nehemiah knew how to confront a difficult problem with decisive action.

Drawing on recent examples of financial fiascoes in the news, what are some of the potential effects of financial misconduct on businesses, ministries, employers, and employees?

_____

_____

_____

_____

In your own realms of leadership, how confident are you in the people responsible for the finances? Do you feel as though you're aware of the details enough to keep people accountable? How much oversight is enough?

_____

_____

_____

_____

Following the financial fiasco, the next serious problem that caught Nehemiah's attention was a *secularized Sabbath*.

 Read Nehemiah 13:15–22.

According to the Jewish calendar, the Sabbath—Saturday—was to be a day of rest in observance of the example set by the Lord when He rested after creating the world. This practice was written in the Law of Moses, and it was also repeated as part of the covenant the people signed in Nehemiah 10:31. How quickly they had returned to conducting business as usual (13:15–16)! No holy Sabbath, no spiritual distinction in their weekly schedule, no fulfill-ment of their promises—only a people who could hear a bargain from a mile away, but who were stone deaf to God's commands.

But Nehemiah hadn't forgotten the people's promise, and he wasn't about to let them forget it. He reminded them of the consequences their forefathers had endured because of their failure to follow through on their commitments to the Lord (Nehemiah 13:17–18). And then Nehemiah set up obstacles and incentives to hold the people to their word (13:19–22).

In Nehemiah 13:17–22, how did Nehemiah decisively correct the problem of profaning the Sabbath? List the practical steps he took to discourage the people's old habits and to encourage new ones.

_____

_____

_____

_____

_____

Finally, Nehemiah confronted a *domestic disobedience.*

 Read Nehemiah 13:23–31.

This domestic disobedience was perhaps the more dangerous and difficult problem of all. Many Jews had intermarried with the pagan people around them. The result was a mixing not only of blood, but of languages and beliefs as well (Nehemiah 13:23–24). Israel was rearing a generation of children who could not speak or understand the language of the Scriptures. This problem threatened to wipe out Israel's ability to hear the voice of the Lord.

For Nehemiah, the greater the problem, the greater was the intensity of his response (Nehemiah 13:25–31). And there are few stronger passages in the Bible concerning confrontation than Nehemiah 13:25: "So I contended with them and cursed them and struck some of them and pulled out their hair." Nehemiah erupted in righteous anger when he discovered Israel's seemingly irreversible error. Israel had experienced judgment for similar offenses in the past, and to avoid God's wrath on the recently restored nation, Nehemiah handed down judgment himself. One commentator notes:

Nehemiah's [response] may seem to be violent and inappropriate for a man of God. However, Nehemiah was concerned that God's judgment not fall again on Judah. He knew God would not tolerate this sin.[3]

In today's language, Nehemiah responded with action similar to that of a CEO who has just discovered that his managers committed offenses that could take down the entire corporation. The appropriate response would not be demotion, lay-off, or early retirement. Nehemiah fired the offenders and showed no partiality or regard for their person or position (Nehemiah 13:28).

If you've ever had to terminate a person's employment or to ask a person to step down from his or her position, describe the most challenging aspects of that decision. Did you take decisive action? What would you do differently if you had to do it again?

_____

_____

_____

_____

STARTING YOUR JOURNEY

Nehemiah followed four basic steps as he dealt with Israel's problems. First, *he faced the sin head-on.* Second, *he condemned it severely.* Third, *he worked toward a permanent correction.* Fourth, *he followed up the situation with prayer.* And though most of the specific problems in Nehemiah's day are unlikely to affect us in our own realms of leadership, the steps he took in addressing problems can be applied to many common issues today.

Recall the specific problem you identified at the beginning of this lesson, and note it in the following space. If this lesson has surfaced other related issues you may have overlooked, list those as well.

Let's take a moment to consider three principles from our lesson that will guide us as we seek to follow Nehemiah's example of leadership.

First, *dealing with problems begins with honest observation.* You cannot solve a problem that you haven't identified. We must force ourselves to face the truth of our own compromising alliances, areas of selfishness, or failure to keep our word, no matter how painful the truth. Once we have removed the sin from our own lives, we will be able to clearly identify the problems in our realms of leadership.

Read Matthew 7:1–5. How might this principle apply to the problem(s) you identified? How might you be looking at them with prejudice, pride, or a biased perspective? How can you correct or clarify your perception of the situation?

Second, *correcting what is honestly observed demands fearless conviction.* Many fears keep us from confronting problems—the fear of what others will think or say, the fear of upsetting the status quo, the fear of being misunderstood. Yet once we have honestly surfaced the problem, we must take a firm stand and do what's right.

What possible fallout might come if you confront the problem(s) you identified? Is your concern about these potential results based on wisdom or fear? Be honest.

_____

_____

_____

_____

Third, *honest observation and fearless conviction must be tempered by consistent devotion.* Nehemiah addressed major problems by focusing on God and the standards of conduct he knew God had commanded in the Law of Moses. Prayer was not a cop-out for Nehemiah, but a vital part of his decisive action. Even when he condemned people with the harshest terms, his anger was tempered by a prayer (Nehemiah 13:29).

Can you think of any Bible passages or biblical principles that seem to apply to the problem(s) you listed earlier? (You may wish to use a concordance to find passages related to certain themes.)

_____

_____

_____

_____

Bring the problems you've listed before the Lord in prayer right now. Take a few minutes to write out your prayer, submitting your own weaknesses and fears to Him. Commit to trusting His will for the outcome.

_____

_____

_____

_____

_____

_____

_____

_____

Now, follow Nehemiah's steps in dealing with the problem. Face it head-on. Condemn sin severely. Work toward a permanent correction. And commit the situation to the Lord in prayer.

What specific course of action will you take to address the problems you identified? Start working on this today.

_____

_____

_____

_____

_____

_____

_____

Appropriately, the book of Nehemiah ends with a prayer: "Remember me, O my God, for good" (Nehemiah 13:31). As Nehemiah obeyed God, he set an example for those under his leadership as well as those outside his realm of responsibility. Though obedience was not always easy, the end result brought blessing. Nehemiah purged the people of Israel from the sin and disobedience that could have destroyed them. And God *did* remember Nehemiah. Not only was that great leader rewarded in his lifetime, but his accomplishments have been eternally recorded in Scripture to inspire us all to greatness in the eyes of our God.

How to Begin a Relationship with God

The key to Nehemiah's outstanding leadership was not his years of experience in a royal court, the skills he learned through an advanced degree, or some mystical hidden talent that made him a "natural." The key to Nehemiah's leadership was *spiritual*—his wisdom, integrity, humility, determination, prudence, discernment, and sense of purpose. All of this flowed from his personal relationship with God.

While Nehemiah exhibits the blessings that come from knowing God personally, let's look at what the rest of the Bible says about beginning this vital relationship with God. The Bible marks the path to God with four essential truths. Let's look at each marker in detail.

OUR SPIRITUAL CONDITION: TOTALLY DEPRAVED

The first truth is rather personal. One look in the mirror of Scripture, and our human condition becomes painfully clear:

There is none righteous, not even one;

There is none who understands,

There is none who seeks for God;

All have turned aside, together they have become useless;

There is none who does good,

There is not even one. (Romans 3:10–12)

We are all sinners through and through—totally depraved. Now, that doesn't mean we've committed every atrocity known to humankind. We're not as *bad* as we can be, just as *bad off* as we can be. Sin colors all our thoughts, motives, words, and actions.

You still don't believe it? Look around. Everything around us bears the smudge marks of our sinful nature. Despite our best efforts to create a perfect world, crime statistics continue to soar, divorce rates keep climbing, and families keep crumbling.

Something has gone terribly wrong in our society and in ourselves; something deadly. Contrary to how the world would repackage it, "me-first" living doesn't equal rugged individuality and freedom; it equals death. As Paul said in his letter the Romans, "The wages of sin is death" (Romans 6:23)—our spiritual and physical death comes from God's righteous judgment of our sin, along with all of the emotional and practical effects of this separation that we experience on a daily basis. This brings us to the second marker: God's character.

GOD'S CHARACTER: INFINITELY HOLY

How can a good God judge the world with the wrath described in Revelation? To bring it closer to home, how can God judge each of us for a sinful state we were born into? Our total depravity is only half the answer. The other half is God's infinite holiness.

The fact that we know things are not as they should be points us to a standard of goodness beyond ourselves. Our sense of injustice in life on this side of eternity implies a perfect standard of justice beyond our reality. That standard and source is God Himself. And God's standard of holiness contrasts starkly with our sinful condition.

Scripture says that "God is Light, and in Him there is no darkness at all" (1 John 1:5). He is absolutely holy, which creates a problem for us. If He is so pure, how can we who are so impure relate to Him?

Perhaps we could try being better people, try to tilt the balance in favor of our good deeds, or seek out methods for self-improvement. Throughout history, people have attempted to live up to God's standard by keeping the Ten Commandments or living by their own code of ethics. Unfortunately, no one can come close to satisfying the demands of God's Law. Romans 3:20 says, "For no one can ever be made right in God's sight by doing what his law commands. For the more we know God's Law, the clearer it becomes that we aren't obeying it" (NLT).

OUR NEED: A SUBSTITUTE

So here we are, sinners by nature and sinners by choice, trying to pull ourselves up by our own bootstraps to attain a relationship with our holy Creator. But every time we try, we fall flat on our faces. We can't live a good enough life to make up for our sin, because God's standard isn't "good enough"—it's perfection. And we can't make amends for the offense our sin has created without dying for it.

Who can get us out of this mess?

If someone could live perfectly, honoring God's Law, and would bear sin's death penalty for us—in our place—then we would be saved from our predicament. But is there such a person? Thankfully, yes!

Meet your substitute—*Jesus Christ*. He is the One who took death's place for you!

> [God] made [Jesus Christ] who knew no sin to be sin on our behalf, so that we might become the righteousness of God in Him. (2 Corinthians 5:21)

GOD'S PROVISION: A SAVIOR

God rescued us by sending His Son, Jesus, to die for our sins on the cross (1 John 4:9–10). Jesus was fully human and fully divine (John 1:1, 18), a truth that ensures His understanding of our weaknesses, His power to forgive, and His ability to bridge the gap between God and us (Romans 5:6–11). In short, we are "justified as a gift by His grace through the redemption which is in Christ Jesus" (Romans 3:24). Two words in this verse bear further explanation: *justified* and *redemption.*

Justification is God's act of mercy, in which He declares believing sinners righteous, while they are still in their sinning state. Justification doesn't mean that God *makes* us righteous, so that we never sin again, rather that He *declares* us righteous—much like a judge pardons a guilty criminal. Because Jesus took our sin upon Himself and suffered our judgment on the cross, God forgives our debt and proclaims us *pardoned.*

Redemption is God's act of paying the ransom price to release us from our bondage to sin. Held hostage by Satan, we were shackled by the iron chains of sin and death. Like a loving parent whose child has been kidnapped, God willingly paid the ransom for you. And what a price He paid! He gave His only Son to bear our sins—past, present, and future. Jesus's death and resurrection broke our chains and set us free to become children of God (Romans 6:16–18, 22; Galatians 4:4–7).

PLACING YOUR FAITH IN CHRIST

These four truths describe how God has provided a way to Himself through Jesus Christ. Because the price has been paid in full by God, we must respond to His free gift of eternal life in total faith and confidence in Him to save us. We must step forward into the relationship with God that He has prepared for us—not by doing good works or being a good person, but by coming to Him just as we are and accepting His justification and redemption by faith.

> For by grace you have been saved through faith; and that not of yourselves, it is the gift of God; not as a result of works, so that no one may boast. (Ephesians 2:8–9)

We accept God's gift of salvation simply by placing our faith in Christ alone for the forgiveness of our sins. Would you like to enter a relationship with your Creator by trusting in Christ as your Savior? If so, here's a simple prayer you can use to express your faith:

> *Dear God,*
> *I know that my sin has put a barrier between You and me. Thank You for sending Your Son, Jesus, to die in my place. I trust in Jesus alone to forgive my sins, and I accept His gift of eternal life. I ask Jesus to be my personal Savior and the Lord of my life. Thank You. In Jesus's name, amen.*

If you've prayed this prayer or one like it and you wish to find out more about knowing God and His plan for you in the Bible, contact us at Insight for Living. You can speak to one of our pastors on staff by calling 972-473-5097. Or you can write to us at the address on the following page.

As you seek to develop your leadership skills, no other decision can compare with the one that puts you in a right relationship with God through His Son, Jesus Christ, who loved us, and gave Himself for us.

Pastoral Ministries Department
Insight for Living
Post Office Box 269000
Plano, Texas 75026-9000

Endnotes

Lesson One

Unless otherwise noted below, all material in this chapter is adapted from "The Matter at Hand," a sermon by Charles R. Swindoll, and supplemented by the Creative Ministries department of Insight for Living.

1. *The New International Dictionary of the Bible*, pictorial ed., ed. J. D. Douglas and Merrill C. Tenney (Grand Rapids: Zondervan, 1987), 718, see "Cupbearer."
2. *The New Unger's Bible Dictionary*, rev. and updated ed., ed. Merrill F. Unger (Chicago: Moody Press, 1988), 267, see "Cupbearer."

Lesson Two

Unless otherwise noted below, all material in this chapter is adapted from "A Leader—From the Knees Up!," a sermon by Charles R. Swindoll, and supplemented by the Creative Ministries department of Insight for Living.

1. Alan Redpath, *Victorious Christian Service: Studies in the Book of Nehemiah* (Westwood, NJ: Fleming H. Revell, 1958), 19–20.

Lesson Three

Unless otherwise noted below, all material in this chapter is adapted from "Preparation for a Tough Job," a sermon by Charles R. Swindoll, and supplemented by the Creative Ministries department of Insight for Living.

ENDNOTES

1. J. Hudson Taylor, *Hudson Taylor*, Men of Faith series (Minneapolis: Bethany House, n.d.), 22.
2. Gene A. Getz, "Nehemiah," in *The Bible Knowledge Commentary*, Old Testament ed., ed. John F. Walvoord and Roy B. Zuck (Wheaton, Ill.: Victor Books, 1985), 675.

Lesson Four

Unless otherwise noted below, all material in this chapter is adapted from "Getting off Dead Center," a sermon by Charles R. Swindoll, and supplemented by the Creative Ministries department of Insight for Living.

1. Winston Churchill, in a radio broadcast, February 9, 1941, quoted in Justin Kaplan, ed., *Bartlett's Familiar Quotations*, 16th ed., ed. Justin Kaplan (Boston: Little, Brown, 1992), 620.
2. Max De Pree, *Leadership Is an Art* (Michigan State University Press, 1987; reprint, New York: Currency Doubleday, 2004), 54.
3. Winston Churchill, first statement as prime minister, House of Commons, May 13,1940, quoted in *Bartlett's Familiar Quotations*, 620.
4. Winston Churchill, speech to the Canadian Senate and House of Commons, Ottawa, December 30, 1941, quoted in *Bartlett's Familiar Quotations*, 621.
5. Winston Churchill, speech to the London County Council, July 14, 1941, quoted in *Bartlett's Familiar Quotations*, 621.

Lesson Five

Unless otherwise noted below, all material in this chapter is adapted from "Knocked Down, but Not Knocked Out," a sermon by Charles R. Swindoll, and supplemented by the Creative Ministries department of Insight for Living.

1. J. Oswald Sanders, *Spiritual Leadership*, rev. ed. (Chicago: Moody, 1980), 177.

2. Cyril J. Barber, *Nehemiah and the Dynamics of Effective Leadership* (Neptune, N.J.: Loizeaux Brothers, 1987), 59–60.

Lesson Six

Unless otherwise noted below, all material in this chapter is adapted from "Discouragement: Its Causes and Cure," a sermon by Charles R. Swindoll, and supplemented by the Creative Ministries department of Insight for Living.

1. John Haggai, *How to Win Over Worry: A Practical Formula for Successful Living* (Eugene, Ore.: Harvest House, 1987), 184.
2. Francis Brown, S. R. Driver, and Charles A. Briggs, eds., *A Hebrew and English Lexicon of the Old Testament* (Oxford, UK: Oxford University Press, 1907; reprint, 1968), 779.

Lesson Seven

Unless otherwise noted below, all material in this chapter is adapted from "Love, Loans . . . and the Money Crunch," a sermon by Charles R. Swindoll, and supplemented by the Creative Ministries department of Insight for Living.

1. Merrill F. Unger, *Unger's Bible Dictionary*, 3rd ed. (Chicago: Moody, 1974), 352.
2. For example, see Ron Blue, *Master Your Money*, rev. and updated ed. (Nashville: Thomas Nelson, 1991), 19.

Lesson Eight

Unless otherwise noted below, all material in this chapter is adapted from "How to Handle a Promotion," a sermon by Charles R. Swindoll, and supplemented by the Creative Ministries department of Insight for Living.

1. Thomas Carlyle, quoted in Justin Kaplan, ed., *Bartlett's Familiar Quotations*, 16th ed., ed. (Boston: Little, Brown, 1992), 413.

2. Francis Brown, S. R. Driver, and Charles A. Briggs, eds., *A Hebrew and English Lexicon of the Old Testament* (Oxford, UK: Oxford University Press, 1907; reprint, 1968), 928–929.
3. Brown, Driver, and Briggs, ed., *A Hebrew and English Lexicon of the Old Testament*, 926–927.
4. *Merriam-Webster's Collegiate Dictionary*, 10th ed. (Springfield, Mass.: Merriam-Webster, 1993), see "integrity."
5. J. Oswald Sanders, *Spiritual Leadership*, rev. ed. (Chicago: Moody, 1980), 99.

Lesson Nine

Unless otherwise noted below, all material in this chapter is adapted from "Operation Intimidation," a sermon by Charles R. Swindoll, and supplemented by the Creative Ministries department of Insight for Living.

1. *Merriam-Webster's Collegiate Dictionary*, 10th ed. (Springfield, Mass.: Merriam-Webster, 1993), see "discernment."
2. *Merriam-Webster's Collegiate Dictionary*, see "prudence."
3. Cyril J. Barber, *Nehemiah and the Dynamics of Effective Leadership* (Neptune, NJ: Loizeaux Brothers, 1987), 99.

Lesson Ten

Unless otherwise noted below, all material in this chapter is adapted from "Revival at Water Gate?" a sermon by Charles R. Swindoll, and supplemented by the Creative Ministries department of Insight for Living.

1. Howard and Phyllis Rutledge, *In the Presence of Mine Enemies* (Old Tappan, N.J.: Fleming H. Revell, 1973; reprint, Carmel, N.Y., Guideposts Associates, n.d.), 30.
2. Augustine, *Confessions*, trans. Henry Chadwick, Oxford World's Classics (New York: Oxford University Press, 1998), 1.

3. Adapted from Insight for Living, *Taking a Stand: A Reformation in Christian Living Workbook* (Plano, Tex.: Insight for Living, 2004), 21–23.

Lesson Eleven

Unless otherwise noted below, all material in this chapter is adapted from "The Fine Art of Insight," a sermon by Charles R. Swindoll, and supplemented by the Creative Ministries department of Insight for Living.

1. Alfred Lord Tennyson, quoted in Justin Kaplan, ed., *Bartlett's Familiar Quotations*, 16th ed., (Boston: Little, Brown, 1992), 455.
2. Francis Brown, S. R. Driver, and Charles A. Briggs, eds., *A Hebrew and English Lexicon of the Old Testament* (Oxford, UK: Oxford University Press, 1907; reprint, 1968), 968.
3. *Merriam-Webster's Collegiate Dictionary*, 10th ed. (Springfield, Mass.: Merriam-Webster, 1993), see "insight."
4. E. D. Isaacs and J. B. Payne, "Feasts," *The International Standard Bible Encyclopedia*, vol. 2, *E–J*, ed. Geoffrey W. Bromiley and others (Grand Rapids: Wm. B. Eerdmans, 1987), 293.
5. J. Oswald Sanders, *Enjoying Intimacy with God* (Chicago: Moody, 1980), 12.

Lesson Twelve

Unless otherwise noted below, all material in this chapter is adapted from "Four Dimensional Praying," a sermon by Charles R. Swindoll, and supplemented by the Creative Ministries department of Insight for Living.

1. *Peanuts*, April 3, 1968, by Charles M. Schultz. Copyright © United Feature Syndicate, Inc. Used by permission of United Media. All rights reserved.
2. Cyril J. Barber, *Nehemiah and the Dynamics of Effective Leadership* (Neptune, N.J.: Loizeaux Brothers, 1987), 131–132. Gene A. Getz, "Nehemiah," in *The Bible Knowledge Commentary*, Old Testament

ed., ed. John F. Walvoord and Roy B. Zuck (Wheaton, Ill.: Victor Books, 1985), 690.

Lesson Thirteen

Unless otherwise noted below, all material in this chapter is adapted from "Putting First Things First," a sermon by Charles R. Swindoll, and supplemented by the Creative Ministries department of Insight for Living.

1. Francis Brown, S. R. Driver, and Charles A. Briggs, eds., *A Hebrew and English Lexicon of the Old Testament* (Oxford, UK: Oxford University Press, 1907; reprint, 1968), 989.
2. Keith Miller, *The Taste of New Wine* (Waco, Tex.: Word Books, 1973), 79.

Lesson Fourteen

Unless otherwise noted below, all material in this chapter is adapted from "The Willing Unknowns," a sermon by Charles R. Swindoll, and supplemented by the Creative Ministries department of Insight for Living.

1. Francis Brown, S. R. Driver, and Charles A. Briggs, eds., *A Hebrew and English Lexicon of the Old Testament* (Oxford, UK: Oxford University Press, 1907; reprint, 1968), 621.

Lesson Fifteen

Unless otherwise noted below, all material in this chapter is adapted from "Happiness Is on the Wall," a sermon by Charles R. Swindoll, and supplemented by the Creative Ministries department of Insight for Living.

1. Philip Yancey, *Open Windows* (Westchester, Ill.: Crossway Books, 1982), 154.
2. Eric Jensen, *Arts with the Brain in Mind* (Alexandria, Va.: Association for Supervision and Curriculum Development, 2001), 14.

Lesson Sixteen

Unless otherwise noted below, all material in this chapter is adapted from "Taking Problems by the Throat," a sermon by Charles R. Swindoll, and supplemented by the Creative Ministries department of Insight for Living.

1. J. W. N. Sullivan, *Beethoven: His Spiritual Development* (New York: New American Library of World Literature, Mentor Books, 1949), 69.
2. Sullivan, *Beethoven,* 62.
3. Gene A. Getz, "Nehemiah," in *The Bible Knowledge Commentary,* Old Testament ed., ed. John F. Walvoord and Roy B. Zuck (Wheaton, Ill.: Victor Books, 1985), 696.

Resources for Probing Further

There's a real shortage today of leaders who are built with the bricklike qualities of Nehemiah. A lot of folks want to cut corners and use lighter materials so they can be recognized more quickly and at a lesser cost to themselves. It's true that bricks aren't as easy to work with as hay and sticks because they're heavy and more expensive. But in the long run, who would say they're not worth the effort?

For further help in constructing your own leadership qualities, here are a few resources we'd like to recommend. Of course, we cannot always endorse everything a writer or ministry says, so we encourage you to approach these and all other extrabiblical resources with wisdom and discernment.

Barber, Cyril J. *The Dynamics of Effective Leadership: Learning from Nehemiah.* Scotland, UK: Christian Focus Publications, 2004.

Barna, George. *Leaders on Leadership: Wisdom, Advice, and Encouragement on the Art of Leading God's People.* Ventura, Calif.: Regal Book, 1997.

RESOURCES FOR PROBING FURTHER

Barna, George. *The Power of Team Leadership: Achieving Success through Shared Responsibility*. Colorado Springs: WaterBrook Press, 2001.

Bennis, Warren and Burt Nanus. *Leaders: Strategies for Taking Charge*. New York: HarperCollins Publishers Inc., 2003.

Blue, Ron with Jeremy White. *The New Master Your Money: A Step-by-Step Plan for Gaining and Enjoying Financial Freedom*. Chicago: Moody Publishers, 2004.

DePree, Max. *Leadership Is an Art*. New York: Currency, 2004.

Finzel, Hans. *The Top Ten Mistakes Leaders Make*. Colorado Springs: Cook Communications, 2004.

Gangel, Kenneth O., *Feeding & Leading: A Practical Handbook on Administration in Churches and Christian Organizations*. Grand Rapids: Baker Books, 2000.

Gardner, John W. *On Leadership*. New York: Free Press, 1993.

Malphurs, Aubrey. *Being Leaders: The Nature of Authentic Christian Leadership*. Grand Rapids: Baker Books, 2003.

Malphurs, Aubrey. *Values-Driven Leadership: Discovering and Developing Your Core Values for Ministry*, 2nd ed. Grand Rapids: Baker Books, 2004.

Redpath, Alan. *Victorious Christian Service: Studies in the Book of Nehemiah*. Old Tappan, N.J.: Fleming H. Revell, 1994.

Sande, Ken. *The Peacemaker: A Biblical Guide to Resolving Personal Conflict,* 3rd rev. and updated ed. Grand Rapids: Baker Books, 2004.

Sanders, J. Oswald. *Spiritual Leadership: Principles of Excellence for Every Believer,* 2nd rev. ed. Chicago: Moody Publishers, 1994.

Swenson, Richard A. *Margin: Restoring Emotional, Physical, Financial, and Time Reserves to Overloaded Lives,* rev. ed. Colorado Springs: NavPress, 2004.

Swindoll, Charles R. *Hand Me Another Brick: Timeless Lessons on Leadership.* Nashville: Thomas Nelson, 2007.

Swindoll, Charles R. *So, You Want to Be Like Christ? Eight Essentials to Get You There.* Nashville: W Publishing Group, 2005.